MARK GUNGOR • JENNA McCARTHY

Treat Them Like Monkeys
By Mark Gungor & Jenna McCarthy

Illustrations by Daria Tarawneh
Book and cover design by dbdesign.graphics

©Copyright 2019 Mark Gungor.
All rights reserved worldwide under the Pan-American
and International Copyright Conventions.

For information, address inquiries to: info@laughyourway.com
www.markgungor.com

Scripture quotations taken from The Holy Bible, New International Version [R]
NIV [R] Copyright [C] 1973, 1978, 1984, 2011 by Biblica, Inc. [TM]
Used by permission. All rights reserved worldwide.
Balloon frame graphics designed by Freepik

Printed in Poland

Wydawnictwo ARKA
Blogocka 28
43-400 Cieszyn, Polska
www.arkadruk.pl

To all the wonderful Monkeys in my life!

Contents

Introduction: Whose Idea Was This Anyway?	**1**
Treat Them Like Monkeys	**11**
Treat Them Like Ducks	**21**
Treat Them Like a Plumbing Leak	**33**
Treat Them Like Mother Nature	**43**
Treat Them Like a Hobby	**53**
Treat Them Like a Marathon	**65**
Treat Them Like Sea Glass	**77**
Treat Them Like an Audience	**87**
Treat Them Like Boomerangs	**97**
BONUS: Do NOT Treat Them Like Royalty	**109**

introduction
Whose Idea Was This Anyway?

There's an old saying by comedienne Phyllis Diller I like to misquote from time to time:

"You spend the first twelve months of your kid's life teaching them to walk and talk, and the next twelve years telling them to sit down and shut up."

I say "misquote" because as I understand it, Phyllis originally said 'you spend the next twelve *months* telling them to sit down and shut up,' but I don't know anybody who managed to get a child to do either of those things in one measly year!

I'm going to tell you something you may not know about me: Of all the things I have been woefully unprepared for in this life—and lo, there have been many—I'd have to put that baffling, exhausting, head-banging phenomenon known as *parenthood* at the tippy top of the list.

No joke: I cannot count the times over the years that my late wife Debbie and I, during our parenting years, looked back and forth from our spawn to each other in genuine confusion and muttered, "Whose idea was this anyway?"

Let's be real about something: It's not like any of us passed any sort of Parental Fitness Test before we decided to start popping out puppies. And speaking of puppies, have you ever tried to adopt one—an unwanted, unwashed one from the pound even? If you haven't, I'm here to tell you that it *is not a fleeting endeavor*. Seriously. There are piles of paperwork and mandatory medical tests and "rehoming fees" and sometimes a waiting period and occasionally even a home inspection to determine if you and your household meet the appropriate minimum standards of "pet-parent suitability."

Oh yes, I know people who have been *denied doggy ownership* because their jobs were too demanding, their yards were too small, or there were other critters in the house that the adoption agency deemed "incompatible." Man, that must be embarrassing...Rejected because one's lifestyle is beneath that of a dog? Not dog-worthy?? Really?!?

But if you want to *make a brand-new human being from scratch* and then bring it home to your filthy, rat-infested shoebox of an apartment and proceed to leave it alone for extended periods of time while you travel around your neighborhood selling crystal meth? Knock yourself out! *Nobody is even going to try to stop you!* (Well, if you get caught you'll eventually go to prison, but I'm saying there are no prerequisites.)

And when you consider the fact that these *brand new human beings* are the result of a very enjoyable romp under the covers *(or wherever you do it)* that has nothing at all to do with *bottles and burp cloths and eventual college tuitions*, it's no wonder so many of us are at a loss when it comes to this whole business of child-rearing.

And the family culture we live in today only exacerbates the problem. You see, for thousands upon thousands of years of human experience, people lived around family. Most people lived their entire lives within a few miles of where they were born.

The result: You were constantly surrounded by people who had a vested interest in you and your offspring. A simple walk out the door and you were going to encounter a grandparent, uncle, aunt, or multiple cousins. One of the positives of all that familial interaction was that you were never more than a stone's throw away from people who loved you, who wanted to help you at all costs, and most importantly, who had lots of experience birthing and raising babies.

But that's not the case in our culture today. No, no, no! As soon as feasible, many of us move as far away from our families as conceivably possible. This is great for one's independence, but not so great for marriage and family. Because in this mobile, modern world, *you are on your own*. And when your toddler is coughing and crying all night long, your eight-year-old is struggling in math, or your demon-possessed teenager is getting into constant trouble at school...well, you will quickly learn that being "on your own" is a scary, lonely place indeed. *(A personal word of advice: Live as close to at least one set of grandparents as you can. Having experienced hands nearby can dramatically reduce your chance of self-inflicted harm brought on by mind-numbing offspring syndrome. This also makes for great, cost-free babysitters.)*

Parenting today? It's madness, all of it! Thankfully we do it anyway, or else this planet would be a sad and desolate place and we'd have nobody to come visit us in the nursing home one day.

All of which is to say, if you're bewildered by your babies in particular or puzzled by parenting in general, you are far from alone—and isolation isn't the only issue we face as families. Another part of the problem is this pervasive idea of the "perfect parent" the media is always trying to sell us. I will let you in on a secret here, friends:

THERE iS NO SUCH THiNG AS A PERFECT PARENT.

There are plenty of loving parents, and lots of well-read parents, and more than a few patience-of-Job parents, *but not one of them is perfect.* And the beauty of that is, it's okay! We don't *need* to be perfect! Our job as parents is to guide and instruct, and even as we're failing miserably, we're doing exactly that. ("Here's how *not* to do it, kids!")

That said, whether you're in the trenches with a newborn or walking around on eggshells around a surly teen, within these pages we've laid out a simple, sensible plan for raising fine, upstanding future adults (and keeping your own sanity and sense of humor intact). It starts with *treating them like monkeys.*

Really.

You're going to love it.

Treat Them Like Monkeys

Obviously, my co-author and I chose that metaphor to make you laugh. And the truth is, the original title of this book (and this chapter) was *Treat Them Like Circus Elephants*, but then we considered how circus elephants are trained and a great deal of the time it's awful and brutal and, well, *the exact opposite of how any sane person would ever tell you to treat your children.* So we decided to go with the monkeys.

People most commonly use the expression "trained monkey" in an insulting fashion and in the context of an absurdly simple task. "A trained monkey could do it," they'll say with a scoff (often to their children when referencing things like replacing the roll of toilet tissue or putting the milk away before it spoils). But very little thought is ever given to the fact that monkeys—pint-size primates who can't even speak English—can successfully be taught to do everything from play piano and pick your pocket to serve the handicapped and explore outer space.

What I'm saying is that *training monkeys* cannot be all that simple, folks. But it's done all the time! With overwhelmingly impressive results! Surely there's a secret to it. (It turns out, there is.)

Let's play a little game: Suppose you were gifted a very inquisitive baby *rhesus macaque* and you were tasked with teaching him how to boil eggs. For this example, we'll call your new pet monkey George. Remember, please, that curious little George does not speak English, and up until this point he's never seen an egg or a pot or a stove in his life. I'm no primate-or-egg-boiling expert, but I'll go out on a limb and suggest that the very first step in your lesson plan would be to *show him yourself how to boil eggs.* Remember, your words are meaningless and because of all that curiosity, his attention span is incredibly short. "Eggs," you might say as you hold them up, to begin to familiarize him with the word. "Pot," you'll point to the cooking vessel. "Yum," you might say as you peel away the shell and take your first bite.

At this point, would you pat yourself on the back and congratulate yourself for successfully teaching George how to boil eggs? Of course you wouldn't! You know that there are going to be *lots* of broken eggs, plenty of overcooked ones, possibly some tears and surely the flinging of raw yokes. You're smart enough to understand that teaching is a process; a series of steps; a lesson in repetition. Sometimes we forget that with our kids, don't we? We yell at them, "How many times do I have to tell you X, Y or Z?" when it's clear the answer is "at least one more time than you already have!"

Children aren't pint-sized adults. They are only partially formed beings, and as such *their job is to learn*. All day, every day, it's just that one job. Let me say that again, because it's one of the most powerful parenting mantras you can ever adopt:

A CHILD'S JOB IS TO LEARN

And how do any of us master any new task? Simple! *By making mistakes.*

In discovering the light bulb, Thomas Edison is reported to have said this: "I have not failed 700 times. I have not failed once. I have succeeded in proving that those 700 ways will not work." When you go into every interaction with your offspring believing in your heart of hearts that it is his or her job to *learn by making mistakes*, your entire relationship will transform.

"He drew on the sofa with Sharpie? He's just doing his job!"

"She talked back to you? She's just doing her job!"

"He lost his library book *again*? Doing his job!"

I'm not suggesting for a minute that there shouldn't be age and crime-appropriate consequences for our children. In fact, there absolutely *must be*, and we'll get to the importance of these in greater detail later. What I'm saying is that training children, like training monkeys, involves bottomless patience and tolerance for mistakes. The more of both you can muster, the happier you'll all be. *(Don't worry, I'll be telling you how to cultivate both of those things later in this book!)*

And let me repeat again: *Children are not pint-sized adults!* I remember as a young parent, trying to deal rationally with our two-year-old daughter who was driving me insane. Now, in my pathetic defense, she was the strongest willed child ever to be born on this planet! And independent? If she could have talked at birth, I am sure she would have looked up at us from the hospital crib and with a perfect mobster voice said, "Hey…what are you two looking at?" When it came to crying, this child had one version:

FULL METAL JACKET

I am not exaggerating. You could never tell if she had fallen and broken her arm or if a little fly had inadvertently landed on her hand. No shades of emotional grey with this child – only blistering black-and-white. Honestly, there were days I was sure that at any moment her head would start spinning in circles, spewing projectile vomit à la Linda Blair in the movie *The Exorcist*.

But I digress... back to my story.

So, picture this iron-willed toddler and her exhausted father *(me)* quickly nearing his absolute wit's end. One day I just lost it completely and I shouted at her, "What is the matter with you!?!"

A friend of mine who was visiting at the time happened to be witness to my inglorious meltdown. He simply shook his head and quietly replied with just the perfect amount of sarcasm in his voice, "Wow... she's acting like a two-year-old." Emphasis on the *two*.

My initial emotional response was, "Yeah, she is!" Then the reality of the comment hit me: She *was* a two-year-old! I'll never forget that moment. At first, I felt embarrassed for losing it in front of my friend. But as his words sunk into my tiny little pea-brain, I began to feel a wonderful sense of release. I wasn't a bad parent, and she wasn't a miniature monster. She was just a two-year-old, acting her age.

Sometimes we expect our children to be *more* like adults and *less* like children. That expectation can only lead to great irritation and disappointment.

We would never treat monkeys like anything but monkeys; we understand the limitations they have and the patience it requires to work with the necessary learning curve to teach them. The same is true for our children.

If we treat kids like the works-in-progress that they are, and work at guiding them in age-appropriate ways with age-appropriate expectations, we will all be better (and happier and more successful) for it.

Treat Them Like Ducks

I'm not trying to drop any subtle hints about your kids with all the comparisons to feral animals, I promise. Sometimes the metaphors just work, okay?

Anyway, there's a business book I love called *Leadership Gold: Lessons I've Learned from a Lifetime of Leading* by John C. Maxwell. In the chapter called "Don't Send Your Ducks to Eagle School," Maxwell points out what should be pretty obvious but often isn't, both in nature and in life:

Ducks aren't meant to be eagles.

They don't *want* to be eagles. Ducks are very, very good at swimming and quacking and working together and bobbing around in ponds and generally being ducks. They may be hearty and waterproof and produce the cutest babies you ever saw in your life, but they make lousy eagles.

Likewise, eagles aren't meant to be ducks. They don't *want* to be ducks. Eagles are very, very good at soaring and looking noble and swooping down on their prey from the sky and generally being eagles. They may be lovely and majestic creatures of God and a symbol of patriotism and strength, but they make lousy ducks.

No one would dare argue that a duck is better than an eagle or vice versa. They're simply different. Sort of like your child and, say, *every other child on the planet*. And yet we compare them all the time in subtle and not-so-subtle ways, don't we?

Of course, it's natural to wonder how your child measures up to his or her siblings or peers. In fact, when they're quite young it's only by comparing that you know when your child is or isn't meeting important developmental milestones.

What's *not* natural—or healthy or helpful—

is making them feel like lesser people because of how they stack up, especially as they get older and in ways not related to say, rolling over or feeding themselves with a spoon.

Cases in point: "I never have to tell your brother to clean his room. He just does it." "Your sister always aced her math tests. You must not study as hard as she did." "Why can't you be more like Susie/Sam/the kid down the street?" The reasons *not* to engage in this sort of side-by-side comparing are many and profound.

First, we know for a fact that insults carry far more weight than compliments. Even if you're praising your child's *other* efforts day and night and even if they're glass-overflowing types, it's hard-wired human nature to remember negative comments and events more frequently and in greater detail than positive ones. What this means is *it's the stuff that stings that your child will take with him into adulthood*. Which could lead to many, many years of expensive therapy for the poor kid trying to figure out why "his parents thought he could never, ever do anything as well as his siblings," even if that's not the actual case at all. Negative programming from one's childhood often is all that is required to guarantee a future life of unhappiness, failure or both.

> **WE KNOW FOR A FACT THAT INSULTS CARRY FAR MORE WEIGHT THAN COMPLIMENTS.**

I was fortunate to grow up in a home with a mother who drilled into her children a positive and reassuring message: Even though we were different, with unique talents, gifts and abilities, she always told each of us, "You can do anything just because you are a Gungor!" She repeated this positive *(although not at all accurate)* message to us over and over in countless situations and under varying circumstances. "You can do anything because you are a Gungor!" Honestly, I think I was at least 35 years old before it dawned on me that "being a Gungor" didn't really mean anything. But by that point it was too late. I'd already done all sorts of things simply because *it had been drilled into me that I could.* Like most everyone, I've hit on some hard times, some rocky lows; but each time I wanted to just surrender and give up, I have had my mother's voice in my head saying to me – no, yelling at me, "You can do anything! You are a Gungor!!"

Consider that programming versus the exact opposite experience so many people had growing up. No matter what they did as children, even if it was positive and noteworthy, they constantly heard the voice of a parent, grandparent or even teacher who scolded them with phrases like, "You are such a failure and a disappointment! Why can't you be better?!?" Consequently, as adults, no matter what their talent, education or experiences may be, the rest of their lives are filled with one failure after another. That voice is constantly tearing them down, filling them with doubts for success, and stealing from them any positive hope for their future.

For those raised in criticism, any failure they experience later in life is just a confirmation of their negative programming. They accept that failure as normal, convincing themselves that they should never have tried in the first place.

On the other hand, those raised with positive programming from the get-go actually view any failure as an aberration. They literally doubt their failures and try again.

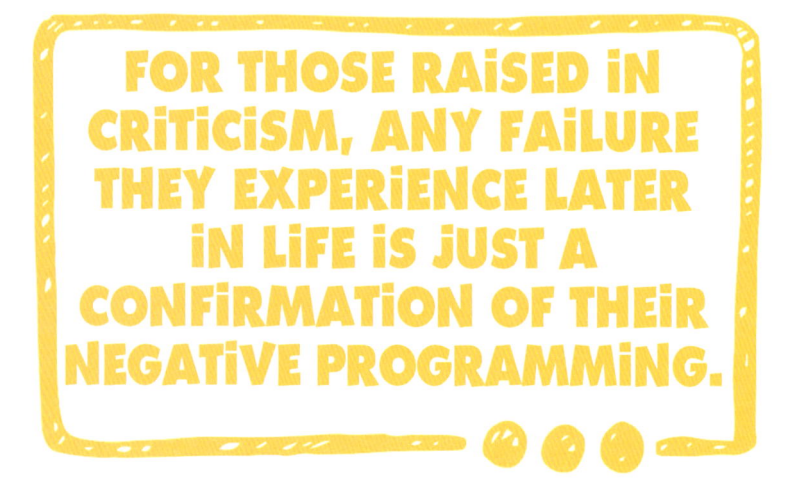

> **FOR THOSE RAISED IN CRITICISM, ANY FAILURE THEY EXPERIENCE LATER IN LIFE IS JUST A CONFIRMATION OF THEIR NEGATIVE PROGRAMMING.**

One of the greatest things about the Christian faith is that, despite any negative programming we may have been raised with, that can all change as we experience God's love. Jesus said, *"Anything is possible with God."* By putting the promises of God into our hearts and minds, we can replace negative programming of the past with positive messages for the future. This is how we begin to doubt our failures and strive for success. The goal with our children, of course, is to fill them with the proper programming right from the beginning, so that they never have to go through the painful undo process.

Beyond not comparing our children to some generic, impossible standard, we also must take care not to measure them against one another. Each of God's creatures has his or her own distinct gifts and talents. Comparing children to their siblings is one of the fastest, most reliable ways to create a rivalrous, contentious, *unhappy relationship* between them. Even the child being compared favorably can't win because he feels burdened with the *pressure to be perfect* all day, every day.

Do you know what it's like following in the footsteps of a studious, mild-mannered, well-behaved, Ivy-league bound sibling? In talking with those who have had that experience, I can tell you it's about as much fun as having a root canal or gargling hot battery acid. More than being "not fun" – it really hurts.

Another problem with constantly comparing your kids to anyone else is *they get used to it*. They learn to see themselves and their place in the world—their very worth—only in relative terms. "I'm prettier than Jane but less successful than Judy." "I'm stronger than Max but he's got more money." This leads to endless feelings of inferiority because guess what? There *always* will be someone thinner/richer/taller/better-at-everything than you. *Always.* It is the happy, well-adjusted person who understands that and loves himself or herself wholeheartedly anyway.

As parents, one of our most important jobs is to help our children discover their *unique* talents and develop them fully and passionately. Doing so boosts self-esteem and increases motivation and success; constant criticizing, on the other hand, increases anxiety and can lead to apathy, depression and bitter, lifelong resentment.

The solution? Don't just let your ducks be ducks; celebrate their waddles! Compliment their quacks! Help them see the beauty and resiliency of their downy coats. Instead of asking them why they can't fly, point out how beautifully they swim.

Encouraging them to be the best ducks they can be is one of the greatest parenting gifts you can ever give—and one that will pay you back tenfold.

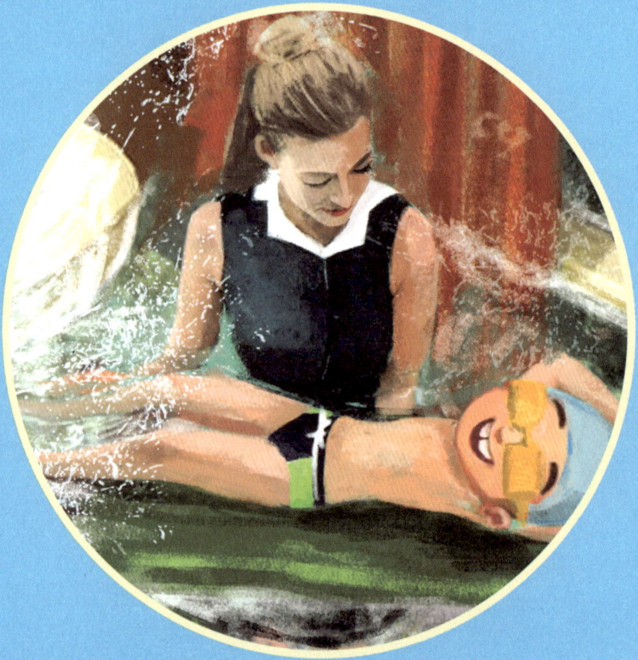

Treat Them Like a Plumbing Leak

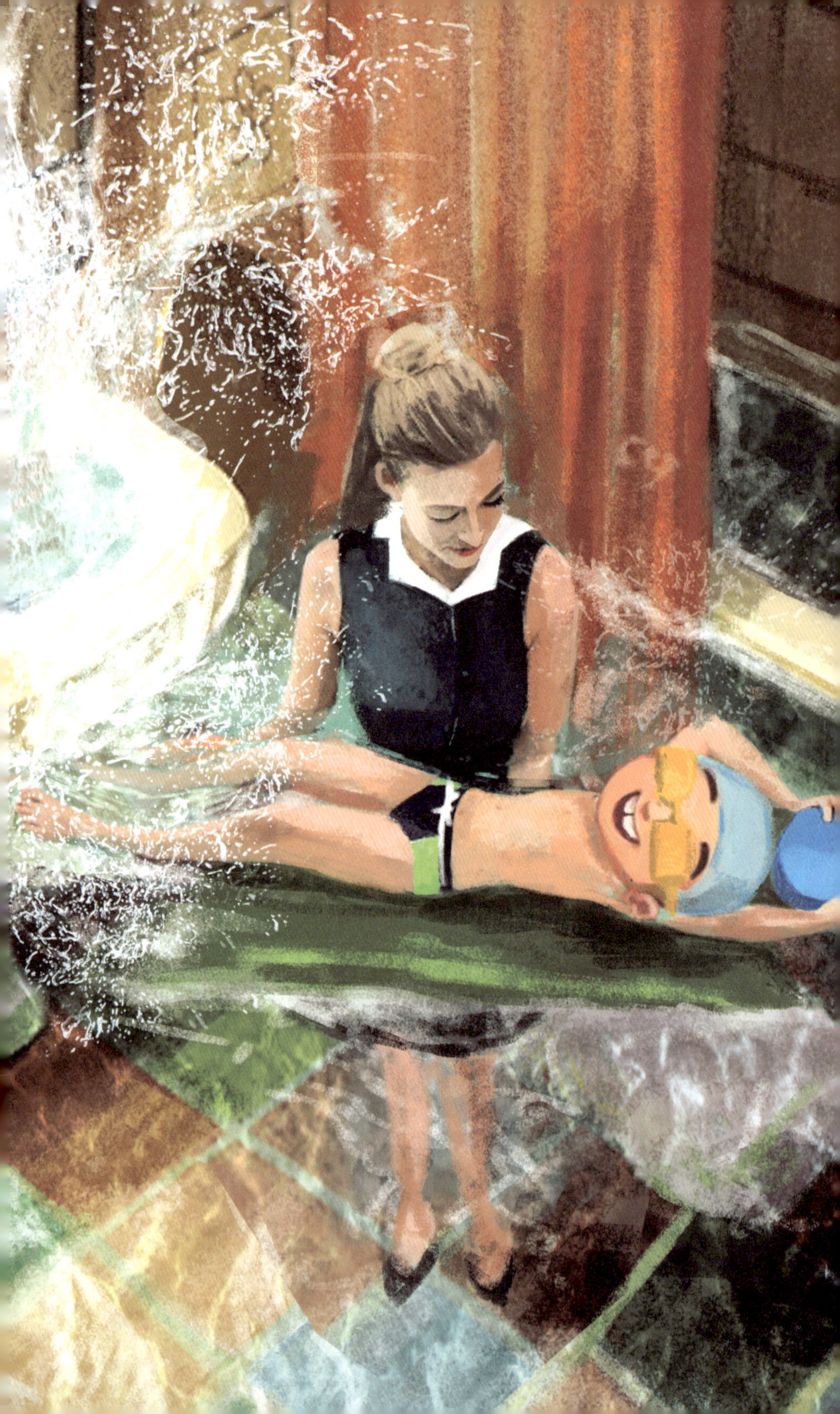

Treat Them Like a Plumbing Leak

Picture the following scenario: You're the last one out of the house and you're running late for work—where you have a Big, Important Meeting. *Missing this meeting is not an option*, just to be clear. As you race past the bathroom, you notice that somebody has left the water running. *Again.* It's just a drip but *drips add up and how many times do you have to tell these people you live with to make sure the water is turned off completely?* You mutter under your breath as you crank the handle, probably a little harder than necessary. Then you watch in slow-motion horror *as the handle comes right off in your hand.*

Water is now shooting out of the faucet straight into the sky at full-force, soaking you, the ceiling, the mirror and basically everything within a four-mile radius.

It. Is. A. Disaster.

Now, let me ask you a very serious question: Of all the many thousands of thoughts floating through your brain at this moment, is any of them this:

"Wow, that's a lot of water but I've got that meeting to go to, so I'll worry about it later."

Unless you're a crazy person,

OF COURSE iT iSN'T!

This leak needs your full attention *right this minute*. Two minutes ago would be even better. Even though you just said very plainly that you could not miss this meeting, now you're going to *miss the meeting*, because

THiS LEAK CANNOT WAiT.

Oh, it *could* wait... but the results would be catastrophic.

Now let me ask you this: When was the last time you stopped what you were doing and put your child or children first?

"I put my kids first *all the time*," you're shouting in your head. "They're the reason I work so hard! They're my life, my *everything!*" And I'm sure they are. But we are all—myself included—occasionally guilty of what I call **Postponement Parenting.**

"Mom, want to hear the song we learned in music today?"

"Dad, want to play chess?"

"Mom and Dad, want to take me out for ice cream?"

I know, I know. These requests come in all day long, most often when we're in the middle of being extremely productive! "Maybe after dinner," we say vaguely, or "We'll play this weekend when we have more time." (*Cue Harry Chapin's *Cats in the Cradle* and grab your Kleenex!)

But what if we didn't postpone? What if we stopped what we were doing—not every time, not even most of the time, but *every once in a while*—and tended to their metaphorical leak? What if we left the dirty dishes in the sink for an hour or skipped our favorite TV show and read a book or played Scrabble or had a water balloon fight instead? Which thing—clean dishes *again* or

AMAZiNG AND SPONTANEOUS QUALiTY TiME WiTH MOM AND/OR DAD

—do you think your child is likely to remember fondly? Which one leaves you with even a tiny chance of feeling regret... and which one doesn't?

Because here's the thing: Modern lives are nuts. Nuts, I tell you! This might be a sweeping generalization, but I also believe it to be true: Most of us are never, ever *not distracted by something*. We walk around, sometimes literally walking into things (I've seen it!) because our faces are in our phones 24/7. We text at the dinner table, play electronic games on the commode and tune into our favorite podcasts as soon as we get into the car.

Imagine trying to be a kid cutting through all that noise? You'd have to spring a *pretty big leak* before getting any attention at all!

We read in the Gospel of Matthew a time when Jesus was pushing his way through a crowd of people. At this point in his short three-year ministry, Jesus was like a rock star. It is said that multitudes of people were gathering around him, listening to his words, watching what he did, reaching out to him with their many personal requests.

In the back of the crowd was a woman who had been very sick for a very long time. She had spent all her money with physicians who only wound up making things worse. She was desperate. She was hurting. She was without any solution to her problems.

She had heard of this Jesus who could make people better. She thought to herself, "If I could just touch his robe as he walked by, surely I could be healed." We don't know how she came to such a conclusion. While Jesus had healed lots of people, there is no record that someone was healed incidentally or in secret. Yet she was convinced that all she needed to do was touch him as he walked by and all would be well with her.

The crowd was pushing against him as he walked to his intended destination. Jesus was focused. He was busy. No doubt his disciples were acting as body guards, making a path through the crowds and pushing back anyone they deemed to be a threat.

As Jesus drew near and was about to pass the woman, she reached out her hand and touched the hem of his garment as he walked by. The Bible records that she was immediately healed. Jesus suddenly stopped and asked what had to seem like a very strange question to the large crowd of people surrounding him: "Who touched me?"

His disciples looked at each other with a degree of confusion and disbelief. They answered, "Who touched you?!? Everybody is touching you!"

But Jesus knew something special had happened. He turned and saw the woman who had been sick. She looked up at him, torn between a sense of fear for drawing attention to herself while at the same time filled with joy knowing that her physical suffering was gone.

No doubt Jesus must have smiled as he looked at the woman and said, "Daughter, your faith has made you well."

The point of the story is that Jesus, despite being very busy and overwhelmed by thousands of people's requests and demands, stopped when he sensed an urgent unmet need; an emergency. He stopped to fix the unexpected leak. Even God stops for emergencies.

Like I said, this isn't all-day-every-day advice. It's plumbing-leak advice. And just like you'll know when you need to *miss the meeting and deal with an urgent disaster,* **if you pay attention to your kids** – and the key here is to pay attention, to slow down, to notice and be sensitive to what they are going through - you'll know when it's time to drop your other duties and give them everything you've got. And you have my word, when you do this you will never, ever regret it.

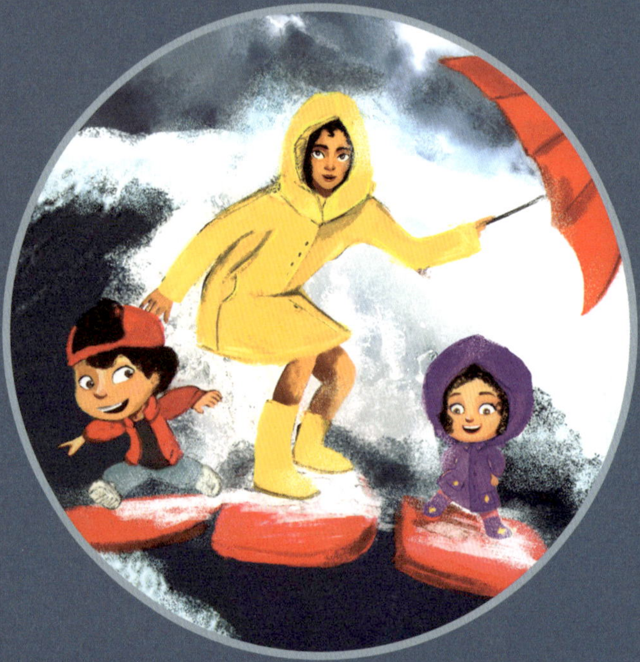

Treat Them Like Mother Nature

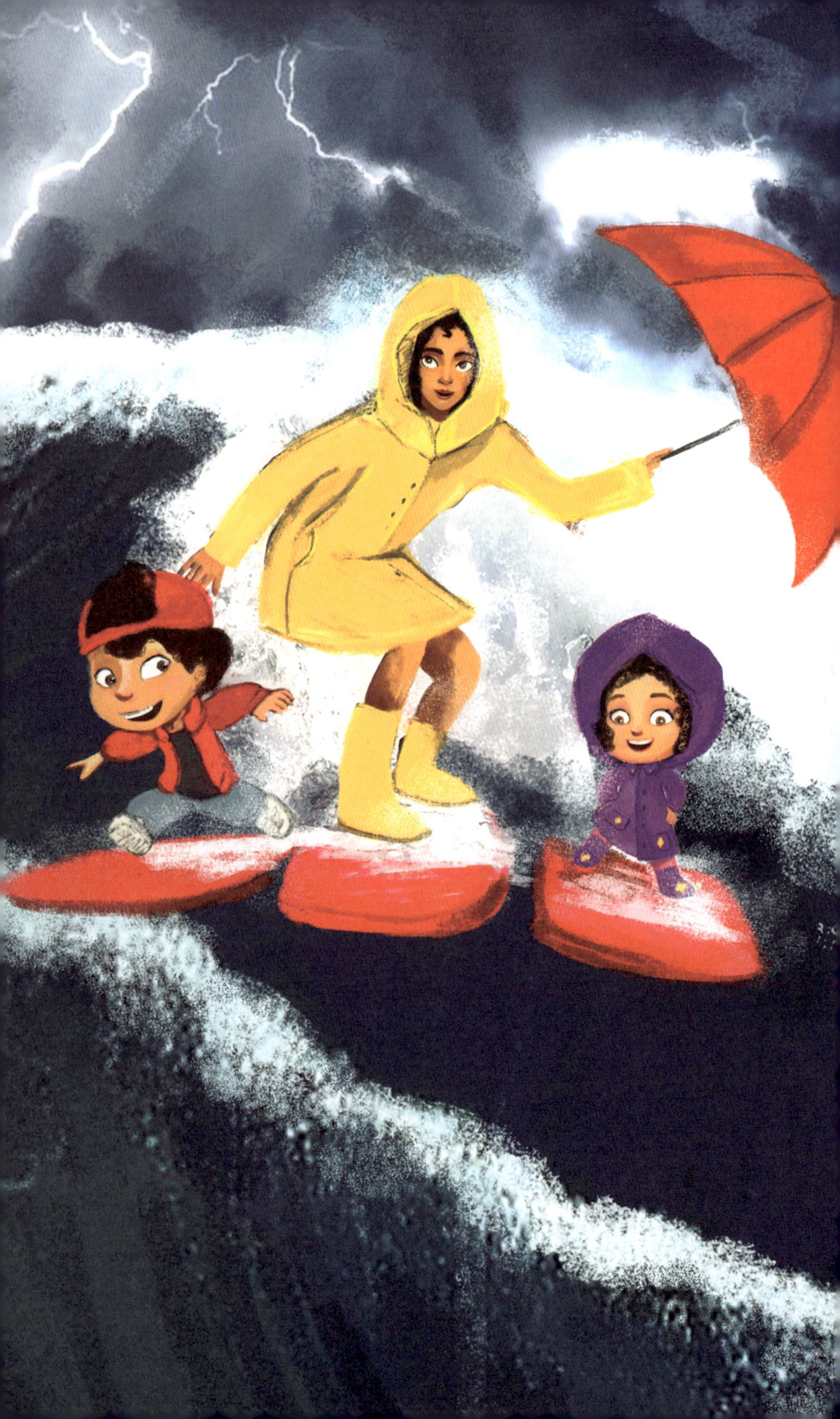

Treat Them Like Mother Nature

You know what's amazing about Mother Nature? *Pretty much everything.*

Think about weather: Sunshine. Snow. Rain. Hail. Hurricanes. Thunder. Lightening. Tsunamis. Tropical storms. Tornadoes. Cyclones. Monsoons. Rainbows. Sure, some of these conditions may make a picnic more pleasant than others, but the very fact that you can have one of them one minute and another the next—*or two of them at the exact same time in the exact same place even*—and that as disparate and dynamic as they are, they can somehow coexist within our earth's delicate ecosystem...that's mind-blowing stuff, if you ask me.

Now consider the plant world: Photosynthesis. Pollination. Cross-pollination. Fertilization. Germination. *Really?* A bee lands on a flower and the pollen sticks to her little feet and then she flies away and *accidentally drips some of that pollen onto another random plant and voila, a new baby seedling is born?* Over and over and over again? Do you even realize how tenuous, how haphazard it all is?

And yet it works. And we know it works, even though we don't always understand *how* it works. We might curse the rain when it's mucking up our commute *(or if you're my wife, our hairdo)*, but we're wise enough to be grateful for it when we see what it does for our lawns and flower beds.

And here's the thing about nature: As often as not, what we consider "bad" weather actually is a gift. Think I'm crazy? Next time there's a tsunami warning, head to your nearest beach and count the hopeful surfers wading in wait. Blizzard about to bear down? Who wants to go skiing this weekend?

My point is, Mother Nature is easy to admire and appreciate in all her hot-headed, unpredictable, even highly destructive glory. So why can't we muster that same awesome appreciation for our children?

The truth is, *we can.* It's not even that hard! All it takes, as philosopher Thomas Kuhn said, is a paradigm shift. Take the know-it-all-teen who's taken to talking back to any adult bold enough to admonish her. Her attitude my not work in your home *(and you're ready with the meaningful consequences to prove it),* but take a step back and you'll see that *her headstrong conviction will serve her well in the world.* She'll be the employee who asks for a raise; the girlfriend who won't put up with emotional games; the tenant who gets the leaky roof fixed ASAP.

Or suppose you have a child who repeatedly walks out the front door without his shoes because his head is somewhere up in the clouds. As frustrating as he may be to parent at this moment, he'll probably never have high blood pressure or worry himself sick about cliques and chicks and fitting in.

The idea is to begin to see your child in the bigger picture of his or her life and its place in the world *(as a storm that will pass)*, and not as he or she is affecting you personally, right now *(think: rain on your parade)*.

The other way weather and children are alike is that they're both as predictably fickle as the day is long. One minute they're bright and sunny and the next they're dark and stormy and you're over there going *"Just tell me if I need sunglasses or an umbrella!"* But even if it rains for sixteen days straight, you know for absolute fact that the sun will come out again.

When you're shoveling snow in Winter, you get through it because you are positive that *wonderful, warm weather is right around the corner.* When you're sweltering in Summer, you remind yourself that cool, *crisp days will be here before you know it.*

The key to succeeding with children is this: Take a long-term view. In other words, *be patient.*

Thankfully, God *(who actually does control Mother Nature)* takes a long-term view of us. **Talk about patience!** Seriously, if I were God, I would have smitten me a long time ago! Why does he tolerate our biggest failures or our worst moments? Because he has a very long-term view when he looks at us. We may be a hot mess today, but he knows that with his kindness and grace in our lives, we can turn into something amazing down the road.

Patience. Yes, that fruit of your loins may seem like a demon-possessed lunatic today, doing things that re-define the word "stupid." But that same lunatic may someday find a cure for cancer, build amazing buildings, solve currently unsolvable problems, visit you in the nursing home and maybe even sacrifice his or her life to save the life of a child.

There is a saying I learned in church a long time ago: I may not be what I ought to be, but thank God I'm not what I used to be. *Patience.*

It may be raining today, but tomorrow could bring a beautiful rainbow.

I ask you: Would you ever dare to expect 70-degree, blue skies 365 days a year? *(Well, you might if you lived in Southern California, but anywhere else you'd be mad!)* You don't just expect those blips and dips on the thermometer; you *prepare* for them. You cover the plants when it snows and you bring in the cushions when it rains, and then you brace yourself and you *get through it*.

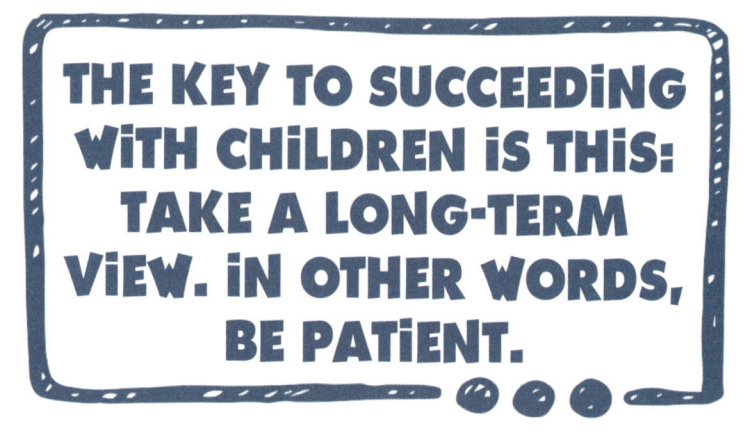

> **THE KEY TO SUCCEEDING WITH CHILDREN IS THIS: TAKE A LONG-TERM VIEW. IN OTHER WORDS, BE PATIENT.**

This same perspective will serve you well at every age and stage of your child's life. As difficult/exasperating/overwhelming/stormy as your offspring may be today, the sun *will* come out tomorrow. *(Next Thursday at the very latest.)*

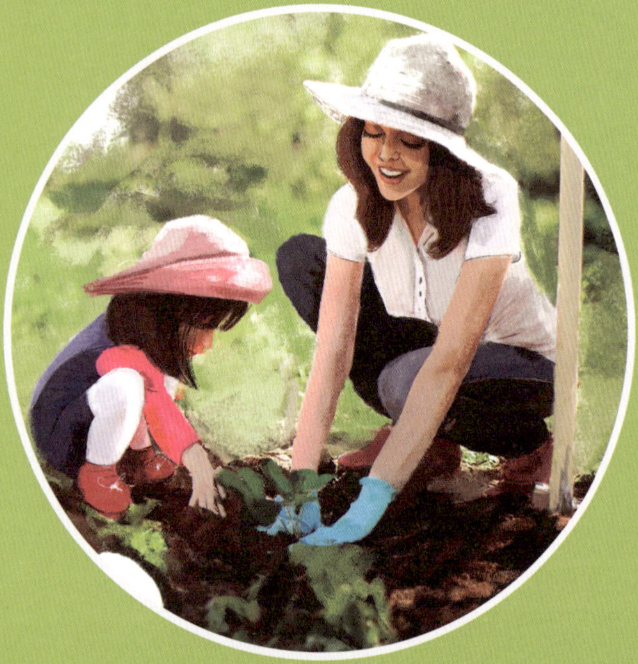

Treat Them Like a Hobby

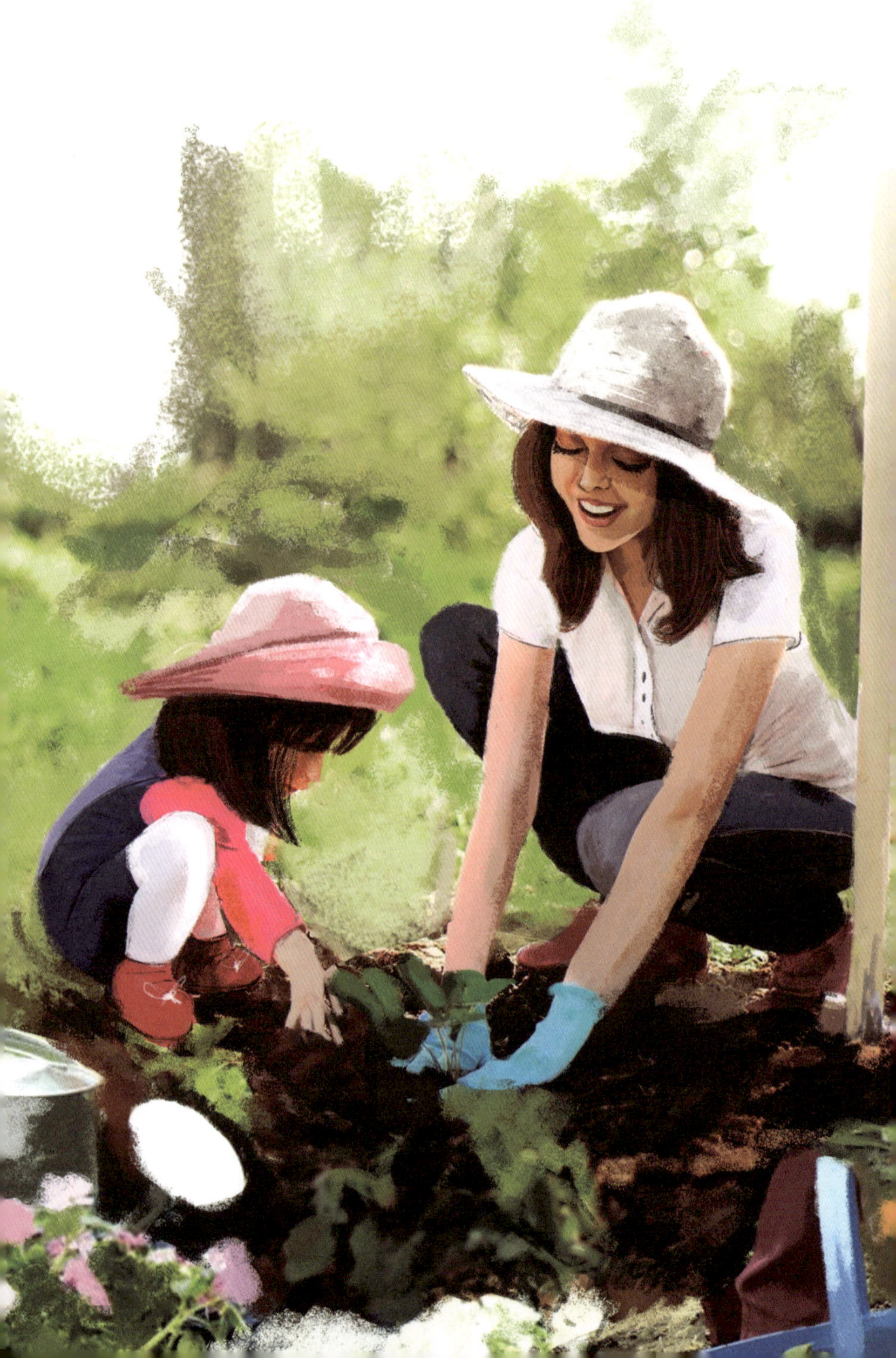

Treat Them Like a Hobby

Nearly every human has a hobby of some form. It might be collecting baseball cards, scrapbooking, reading WWII novels, trout fishing, quilting, Bunco, skeet shooting, or keeping up with the Kardashians. Whatever it is that trips your trigger for leisure activity, there is one thing that is certain when it comes to our hobbies: *We find time for them.*

Let's face it: Life is busy. There's so much we want to do, mixed in with so much that we *must* do.

The problem, of course, is that we all get so busy and caught up in the minutia of our lives that "hanging out with the kids" often gets bumped way—and I mean *way*—down the priority list. And sure, we have to work and pay bills and do all those other grown-up things we do. But most of us also manage to find what likely amounts to several weeks a year to spend time playing around on our phones, trolling Facebook, binge-watching something or other on Netflix or engaging in one of the aforementioned hobbies. I wonder what would happen if we spent some of those weeks with our children instead.

Your kids might tell you that the one thing they want more than anything in the whole wide world is an Xbox or the new iPhone 37 or a unicorn that poops golden rainbows or an official Red Ryder carbine action two-hundred shot range model air rifle *(he'll shoot his eye out, by the way)*, but the truth is, what they really want is your time.

Even if they act like they don't (make that *especially* if they act like they don't—that's a classic kid test to see if they're still lovable even when they're being awful little trolls). Whether it's old-school tossing a football back and forth or playing a card game or just going for a walk together, when you *choose to spend your precious minutes with your children,* you send deafeningly powerful messages of love and admiration.

And make no mistake: *Children who feel loved and admired grow up to be loving, admirable adults.* Who doesn't want to foster that?

You know the most common excuse I hear from guys in particular about why they don't spend more time with their kids? **Work!** And it's true, men have been told that we should give 100% at work.

In fact, many of us believe that's the only way to get ahead. And I agree that we should all be diligent, committed, honest and trustworthy workers. But give 100%? **Really?** If you're giving 100% at work, what do you have left to give at home? I'm no math genius, but I'm pretty sure that would be nothing. Zero. Zip. Nada.

I know, I know...you hear your favorite sports heroes say, "I left *everything* on the field."

Yeah, yeah, yeah, blah, blah, blah... Look, if you leave *everything* you have at your job, you will have *nothing* left for the most important people in your life: **your family.**

The man who gives 100% at work will neglect his children. And neglected children tend to grow up to be damaged, depressive, destructive adults. What kind of success is that?

The man who gives 100% at work so he can become a financial success is only fooling himself. Because when his neglected wife divorces him, she will take half of everything he has achieved. Even from a financial viewpoint, giving 100% at work makes little sense.

> **CHILDREN WHO FEEL LOVED AND ADMIRED GROW UP TO BE LOVING, ADMIRABLE ADULTS.**

Stop with the 100% nonsense. Pace yourself. Even your demi-god sports heroes know that. That's why they take time-outs or go sit on the bench from time to time. If they burn *everything* at the beginning, they will never make it to the end of the game.

When I was in high school I ran for the track team. We trained for hours on end, running and sweating, disciplining ourselves to be the best track team we could be. We had a beautiful outdoor track that we trained on that surrounded the football field. I got familiar with the visual cues of that track and would pace myself just right so I could still have a burst of speed at the end.

On our first track meet of the year, we went out of town to compete against another school. Unlike our school, they had a nice indoor track facility, which, considering we lived in Wisconsin *(home of the 15th coldest city in the entire U.S.)*, was probably a better idea.

Anyway, we looked at their tiny indoor oval track. We would have to run around their little track three times to equal one lap around our standard outdoor track. The problem was, I had no visual cues of how to pace myself on their little gerbil-like track. When the gun went off and the adrenalin started pumping, I took off like a bat out of hell *(Theological question of the day: Does hell actually have bats?)*, leading the pack, running like the wind. Of course, there was no wind because we were running inside, but nevertheless I ran and ran and ran and then BAM!! I hit a wall of exhaustion like I had never experienced before in my life. I began to slow down dramatically and went from being far in the lead to watching every other runner pass me by on their glorious way to the finish line. It was horribly humiliating. I didn't pace myself properly and I ran out of steam before I could cross the finish line.

The Bible instructs, *"Whatever you do, work at it with all your heart"* (Colossians 3:23). But it also tells us not to be idiots. Okay, it doesn't exactly say that. It says, *"fools die for lack of sense"* (Proverbs 10:21). Don't be foolish. Don't give *everything you have* at work. You need to pace yourself. Work hard, but come home with something still left to give.

By the way, these same guys who claim they have to give 100% to their jobs often are the same ones who somehow manage to squeeze in time for hunting or car shows or paintballing. Why? Because it's important to them.

The truth is, the lives of most of the modern-day parents I know, both men and women, are so jam-packed that at least half of their interactions with their children occur in the form of clipped text messages. It's *hard* to carve out an hour or even ten minutes for some quality time together, but remember:

YOU REAP WHAT YOU SOW.

If you show your children that they rank somewhere in between *Law & Order* and your snarky co-worker's Facebook feed, they will likely to grow up into distant, emotionally detached adults. Make space in your life for them...just like you do for your hobbies. Be intentional and carve out time for your kids the same way you do for that fantasy football league or the Pinterest browsing. Give them your time and attention generously and they'll thrive like rubber trees in a rainforest.

> **BE INTENTIONAL AND CARVE OUT TIME FOR YOUR KIDS THE SAME WAY YOU DO FOR THAT FANTASY FOOTBALL LEAGUE OR THE PINTEREST BROWSING.**

Try this one day this week (*or ideally, every day this week*): Set aside a half hour for each of your children and choose an activity you think they'll enjoy. It could be baking cupcakes, walking around the neighborhood, building blocks or playing a board game. *Anything that involves interaction and doesn't involve a screen* will do. Turn your cell phone and laptop off or stow them in another room. Do not answer the phone or respond to texts. Simply give your child your undivided, rapt attention for those one thousand, eight hundred consecutive seconds. I'm going to bet great things will happen.

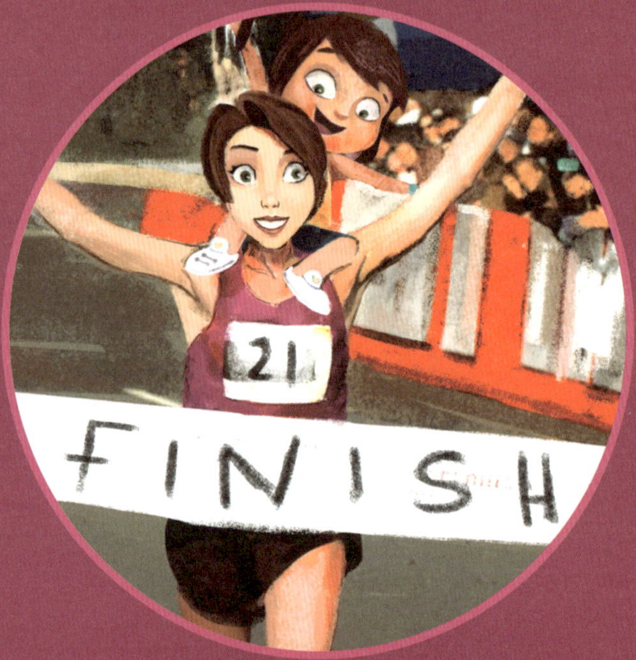
21
FINISH

Treat Them Like a Marathon

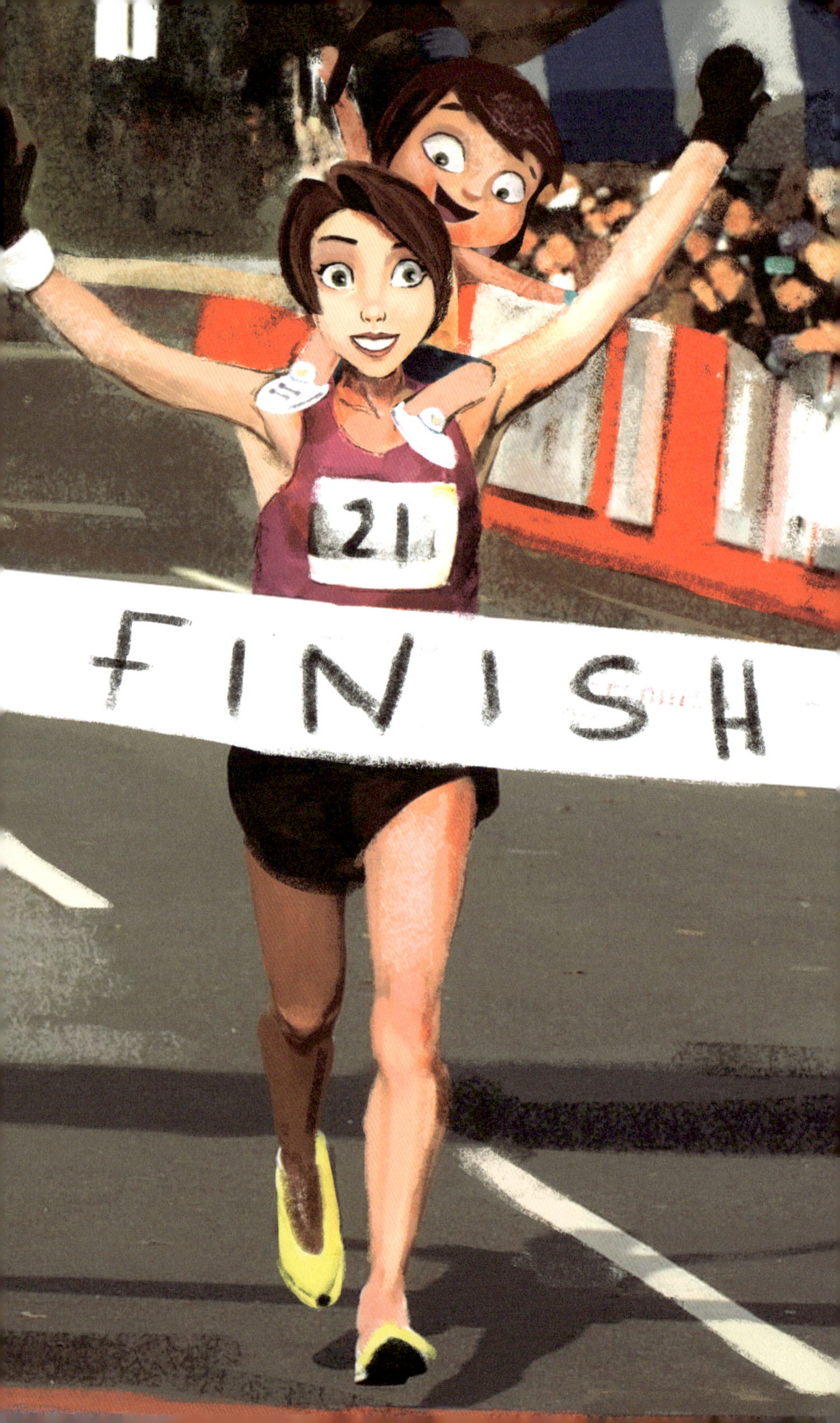
21
FINISH

Treat Them Like a Marathon

I'll be honest. I might have been a track star in high school, but those glory days are way behind me. Unless there's a bear chasing me or West Marine is having a ninety-percent-off sale, you're not likely to catch me running. That's because running is very, very hard and life is short and thankfully, there are other aerobic activities I actually enjoy at this advanced stage in my life *(but that's another book altogether)*. Anyhow, because running is so very, very hard, I have a great deal of respect for people who routinely choose to do it for, say, *twenty-six-point-two consecutive miles*

with no bears and no boating accessories sales involved.

Seriously, that's just crazy to me! But people run marathons all the time! And they're not all elite athletes with big corporate sponsors and two percent body fat, either. No, regular old people like you and me sign up for these ultra-endurance events. And then they train and train and train some more. Are they all trying to win the thing? Of course not. Are they trying to break world records or sprint their way to fame and fortune? Probably not even a handful. I'm guessing ninety-nine percent of marathoners share a singular common goal: To finish the thing.

That's it!

That, my friends, is as apt a metaphor for parenting as I've ever heard. Think about it: We often sign up for this gig sort of on a whim and without a concrete understanding of what's really going to be involved. We may be vaguely aware that there will be pain and heartache and sleepless nights and a lot of money and poop involved, but we brush those notions right under the rug.

"People do it all the time," we chirp. "How hard can it be?"

Let me let you in on a little secret: It can be *really hard*. Like, running-a-marathon-uphill-in-banana-slippers-and-carrying-a-porcupine hard. But think about that marathon for a second. What happens if you give up? Then you didn't run a marathon! Even if you make it twenty-five miles before quitting, you don't get the medal, or the accolades, or the bragging rights. You either cross the finish line or you don't; it's that simple. All that training, the hard work, the sacrifices... for nothing. I don't know about you, but if I actually got myself out there on the course, I'd be hell bent on finishing that race, even if I had to crawl over the finish line on bloody hands and knees to do it.

My hard-earned advice to parents, especially those in the teenager-trenches, is this:

DON'T STOP PARENTING TOO SOON

This is the great temptation that dangles itself in front of every parent. Let's face it, year after year this kid has needed your constant attention, and it has been exhausting. Now they can dress themselves, feed themselves, maybe even drive themselves. It's tempting to quit parenting too soon. Oh, these AWOL parents don't say it like that. They use lofty, feel-good phrases like, "I trust my kids." *(By the way, if you trust a teenager – you are a moron. When I was a teen we LOVED going to the homes of the parents that "trusted" their kid. That's where all the booze, drugs and sex went down!)*

I was speaking at a church on the West Coast not long ago. During one of the breaks, I found myself talking to this pastor who was enjoying the conference. He was showing me some family pictures and pointed out his teenage daughter. She. Was. Gorgeous. One of those 15-year-olds who look at least 21. I said, "Wow. She is stunning. Is she here with you and your wife?"

"Oh no," he replied. "She's at home with her boyfriend."

"Alone?" I queried.

"Yeah," he laughed. "They usually spend all day on Saturdays in her bedroom with the door closed, working on homework."

I was stunned. How stupid could this guy be? I'm sure they were studying alright – and I bet it had more to do with anatomy than mathematics. My wife and I watched our teens like hawks surveying their prey. It would have been a cold day in hell before they could lock themselves in their bedrooms with someone of the opposite sex. We told our kids that no one of the opposite sex is EVER allowed into their bedrooms. My son asked, "What if there is a fire and the only one who can save me is a girl?" I replied, "Then you are going to die."

The parents who quit on the job are the ones who are shocked when their tenth-grade daughter gets pregnant or their eleventh-grade son gets arrested for shoplifting. They're the ones who didn't see it coming when their twelfth-grader gets suspended for selling drugs, or their ninth-grader comes home drunk from a party *(the one he told you would be supervised but clearly wasn't)*.

They're the parents who are "too embarrassed" to talk about the dangers of promiscuity or underage drinking; the ones who turn a blind eye to the early warning signs *(and there are plenty!)* of a troubled teen.

The parents who quit on the job are the ones who get a call from the police about something illegal their kid was caught doing. "But she said she was just going to hang out at her friend's house," they cry. But did they ever check to make sure that's exactly where she went? Did they call the parents of said friend to check on how things were going? Do they even know what type of person this so-called friend really is? No, no, no. They were busy jumping off the parenting ship while it was still moving!

Parenting is hard. It's so hard for so long that I've seen far too many parents get their kids to their teen years and then just give up. "If he doesn't know right from wrong by now, he's *never* going to get it through his thick skull," they say of their sixteen-year old. Or "I taught her everything I know, now it's her turn to exert her independence." While both statements may be unarguably true, at the risk of offending anyone, they're the words of quitters! You need to stay connected, involved and vigilant. As long as your offspring can benefit from your guidance and support and yes, your occasionally stern and vocal disapproval, the race is still on.

> **YOU NEED TO STAY CONNECTED, INVOLVED AND VIGILANT.**

I'll let you in on a little secret, too. These older kids? The ones who seem so able-bodied and self-sufficient? The very ones who insist on a daily basis, "I got this, Mom and Dad"? *They are often the ones who need your wisdom and leadership the most.* And when they storm through the house shouting, "I don't want to talk about it!" I want you to take that not as a fact, but as a challenge. Part of the natural separation process is for kids to *think* they can do everything without your help. And eventually they will be able to... as long as you don't prematurely jump off the parenting ship.

Let's face it, kids can suck the life out of you. But guess what? It's only for a relatively brief and thankfully finite amount of time, and let me point out, *you signed up for this race.* Just because they can brush their own teeth and don't poop their pants anymore doesn't mean you can check out. You need to keep connected. Remain vigilant. Stay engaged. You're not done until you cross the final finish line and can finally rest in peace (you know, because nobody is talking back to you or worrying you sick anymore). Stay the course! You'll be glad you did. It will be the most rewarding (and exhausting) race you will ever run.

> **YOU'RE NOT DONE UNTIL YOU CROSS THE FINAL FINISH LINE.**

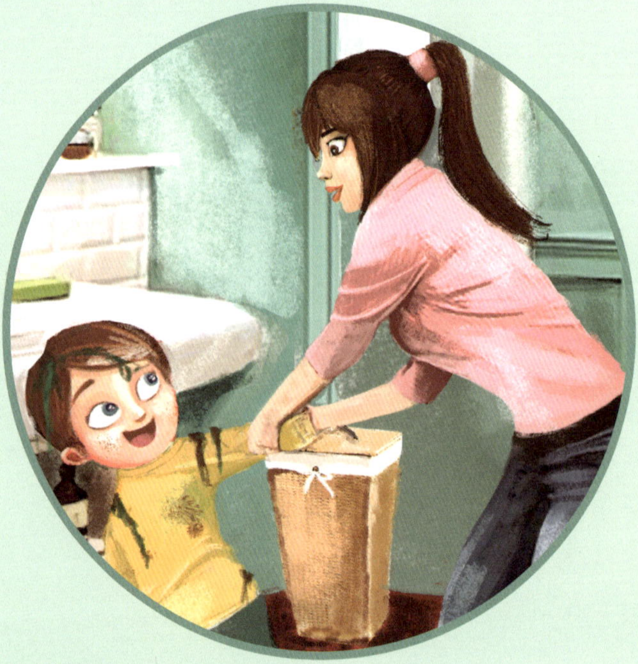

Treat Them Like Seaglass

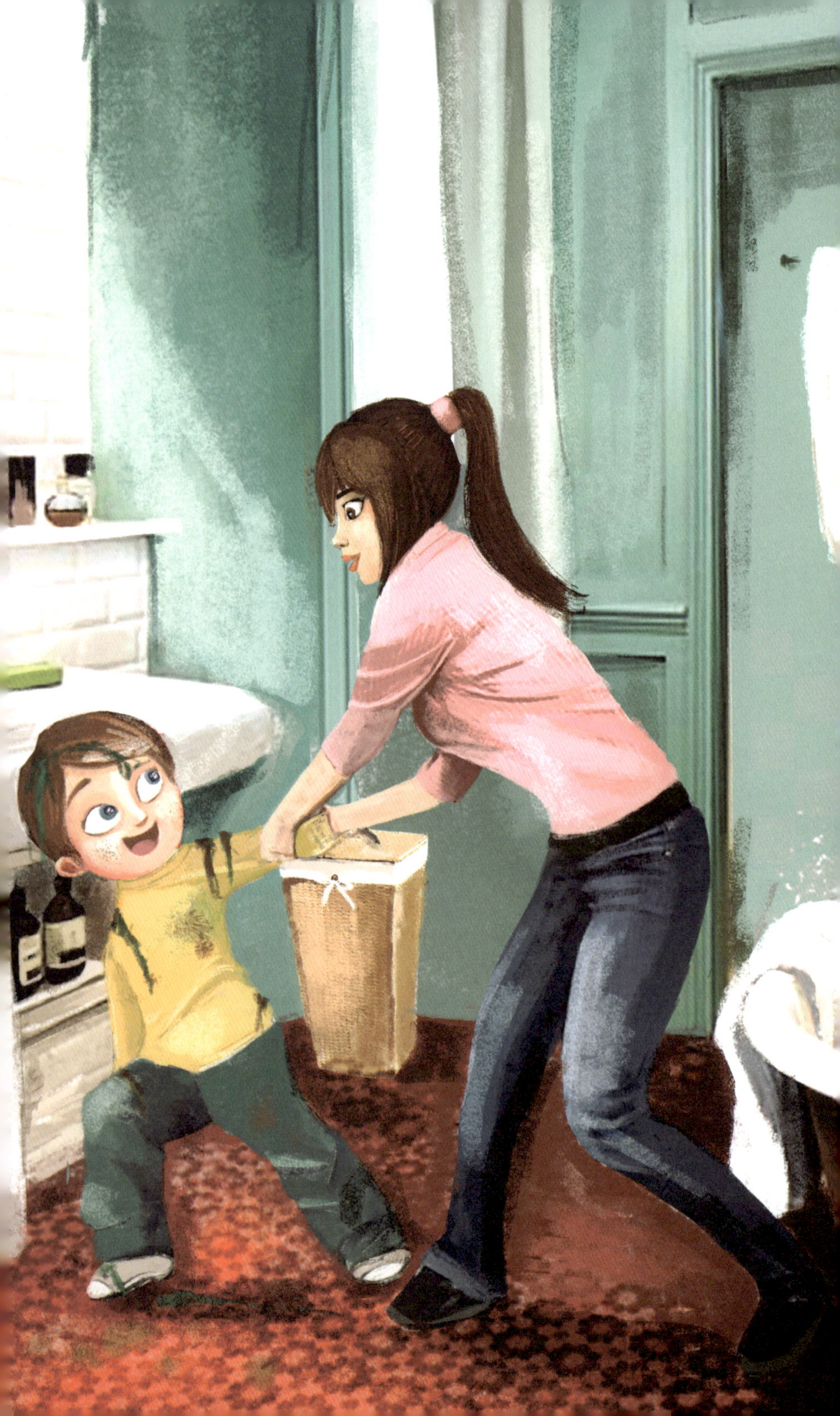

Treat Them Like Sea Glass

I travel constantly, and one of my favorite things to do whenever I'm in a coastal town is comb the local beaches for sea glass. I find it very soothing, not to mention a wonderful way to enjoy the local landscape in a mindful and meditative way.

Sea glass starts out as normal shards of broken glass from bottles or even shipwrecks. These shards of glass are rolled and tumbled in the ocean for years and years until all their edges are rounded off and the slickness of the glass has been worn to a frosted appearance.

Over the years there's something I've discovered about sea glass: It's always there. *Always.* Some days and in some locations, it can seem harder to find but if you look long and hard enough, it's always, unquestionably there. Of course, sometimes the beach is covered in seaweed or tar...or you get distracted by the sailboats gliding by...or your wife asks you to grill thirty or forty hamburgers for a few of her closest friends... or you're tired and you just don't feel like scouring the shoreline for bits of broken beer bottles! The fact is, lots of things can get in the way of the sea glass hunt if you let them.

But guess what? That sea glass is still there. The thing is, I believe sea glass is a perfect metaphor for the good in your children: *It's always there.* Always. But as perfectly imperfect creatures, sometimes your kids are covered in tar. And in those tar-covered moments, you're not thinking about their beautiful, shiny sea glass-bits. *You need to do something about that tar!* You need to point it out! Remove it immediately! Pontificate swiftly and deeply your own hard-earned tar-avoidance strategies! In other words, *you need to focus on the bad.* Hey, you're just doing your job!

The problem is that all of us—but kids especially—react to the negative way more strongly than we react to the positive. It's just human nature. I can't count how many times I've heard a kid say, "My parents criticize every single thing I do!" or "I can't do *anything* right!" While these are (hopefully) exaggerations, to the child in question that's exactly what it feels like when you're over there just "doing your job."

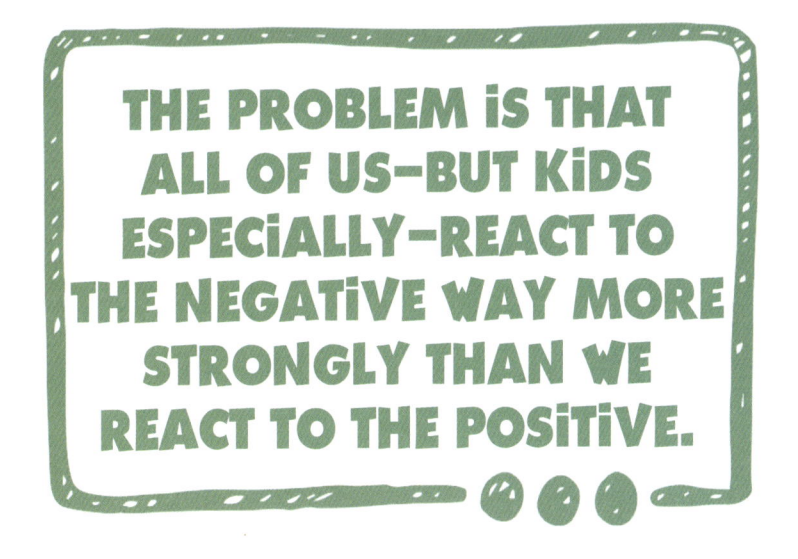

> **THE PROBLEM IS THAT ALL OF US—BUT KIDS ESPECIALLY—REACT TO THE NEGATIVE WAY MORE STRONGLY THAN WE REACT TO THE POSITIVE.**

The solution? Look for sea glass! Remember, it's always there, even after a devastating oil spill. Instead of only looking for ways you can guide or instruct or otherwise help your child improve, shift mental gears every once in a while and find something fabulous in him or her and point it out.

TELL HiM WHAT HE'S ALREADY DOiNG RiGHT!

"I really appreciate that you made your bed without me asking," you might note. "I'm proud of how nicely you're sharing with your sister." "You've worked so hard on your spelling, it's really paying off!"

The reason it can be so difficult to complement your children is because…well…you know they can do better!! But if you constantly point out where they fall short, they will become discouraged and want to give up altogether.

Ephesians 6:4 says, *"Fathers, do not exasperate your children…"* When I first read those words I thought, "Wait a minute… isn't this backwards? Aren't the children the ones who exasperate the fathers?!?" Even Webster's dictionary uses the following sentence to illustrate the word exasperate: "...small children can *exasperate* their parents with endless questions about why this or that..."

See?!? It's the children who do the exasperating!

But the Bible has it right: We are the ones who should take care not to do the exasperating. You see, when children do the exasperating, it is just an exhausting experience for the parent. But when the parent does the exasperating – constantly pointing out the child's shortcomings and failures – then great damage can be done to the child.

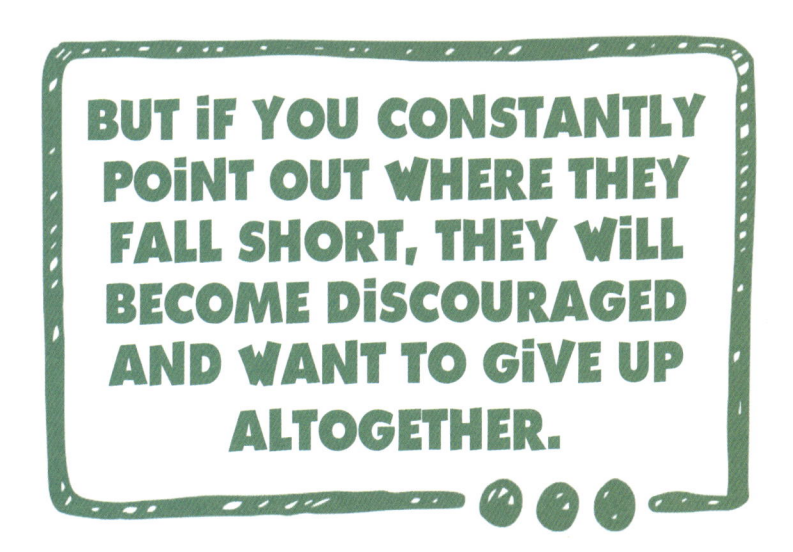

> BUT iF YOU CONSTANTLY POiNT OUT WHERE THEY FALL SHORT, THEY WiLL BECOME DiSCOURAGED AND WANT TO GiVE UP ALTOGETHER.

Our goal as parents is to build our children into confident, productive, well-adjusted adults. Would you try to build a building by constantly tearing it down? Adding one brick and then taking away two? Of course you wouldn't! Psychologists say it takes five positive comments or interactions to outweigh the pain of just a single negative one. Think about that! Every time you scold, punish or even redirect your child—even if all those actions are both deserved and appropriate—it takes five compliments, acknowledgments, "atta-boys" or high-fives just to get back to neutral.

For the record, I'm not suggesting we all start mollycoddling our kids and letting them run roughshod over us by overlooking the bad and telling them they're wonderful around the clock. Quite the contrary! I'm a huge fan of discipline—heck, the word discipline has *disciple* right in it! I'm simply reminding you, as a fellow parent who's been in the tar-removal trenches for several decades now, that it's important never to lose sight of the fact that our kids are mostly good (even when they're acting like little jerks). Nobody ever found a treasure trove of sea glass quite by accident. What you look for, you will find.

> **PSYCHOLOGISTS SAY IT TAKES FIVE POSITIVE COMMENTS OR INTERACTIONS TO OUTWEIGH THE PAIN OF JUST A SINGLE NEGATIVE ONE.**

Look for the good in your kids. I promise you, it's always there.

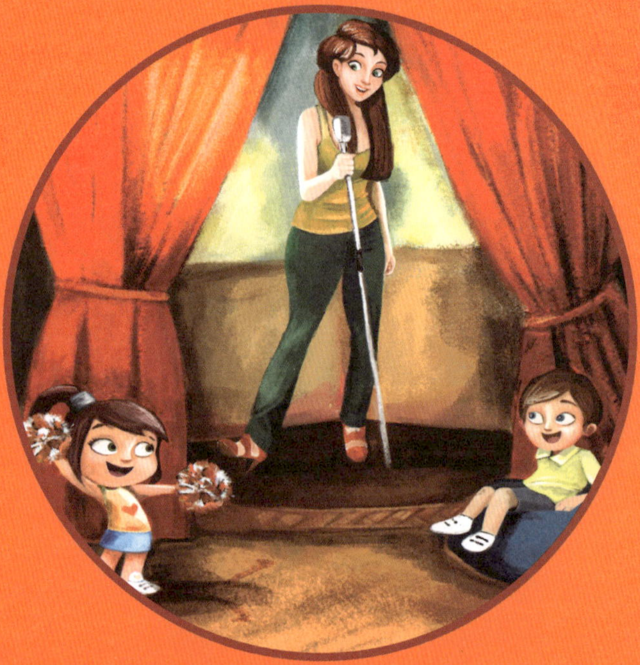

Treat Them Like an Audience

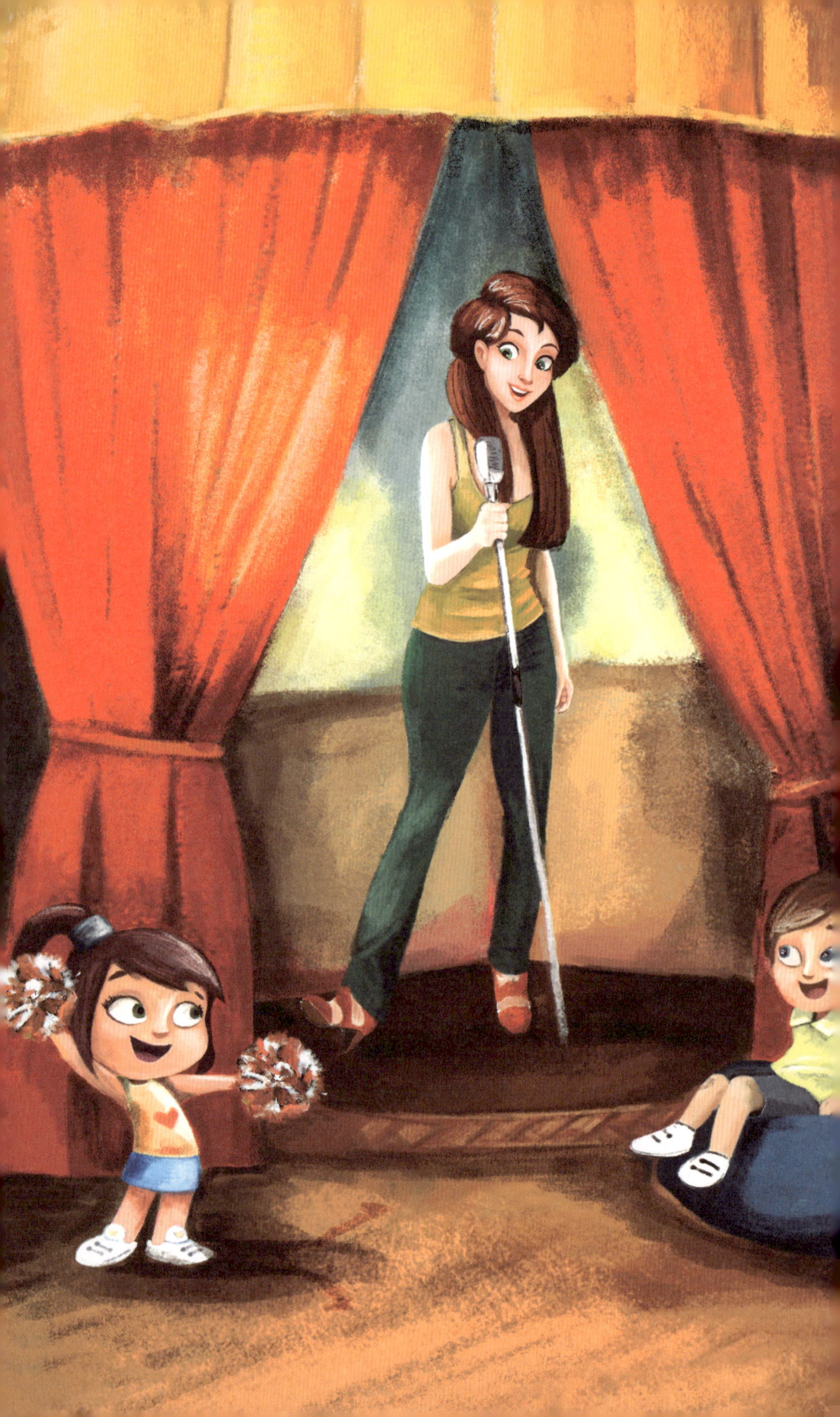

Treat Them Like an Audience

Quick, dumb question: When you go to the theater, what do you do *(besides, if you're a man, grumble at your wife about dragging you to the theater or the price of the tickets or both)*? You watch the stage! Intently! Do you ever, just for fun, squeeze your eyes shut as tightly as you can and try to just *listen* to the play? I'm going to guess that you don't. And why is that? Because one character might be whispering "I love you" as he slits another's throat; a burglar could be silently ransacking an apartment; a child could be promising her parent she didn't break the lamp...but only the audience can see she's got her little fingers crossed behind her back. You need to *watch* the play to really take it all in. After all, everybody knows that actions speak louder than words.

Whether you realize it or not and whether your kids are two months or two decades old, your offspring are your audience 24/7. They are watching you—intently, I might add—and as the saying goes, "they're far too busy minding every move you make to listen to a word you say." Of course, if your actions are backing up your words, then you're good to go. But if you're standing on your soapbox telling your son to be honest and kind and to treat his body like a temple while you're cheating on your taxes, kicking the dog and smoking a cigarette, which messages do you think he's going to get?

Children are desperate for role models, despite their occasional *(read: incessant)* "I got this" posturing. The way you treat your waitress, or the person who accidentally spills your coffee in Starbucks, or your spouse for that matter, is how *they're* likely to treat these people someday. If you have a child over the age of five or so, you already know this to be true, because by then you'll have heard her playing with her friends or her baby dolls and bark a tiny command that very well could have come out of your own mouth.

***(Confession:** My own ah-ha moment of this nature came in a grocery store parking lot when my grown son was just a toddler. I was waiting patiently (ahem) for another car to back out of the choice parking spot I wanted when a third car turned into the row from the other end. I had no idea my young son was paying attention to any of this—or understood even an iota of the diplomatic nuances of driving for that matter—but as soon as that car appeared in his line of vision he immediately piped up from the back seat, "Don't even **think** about it, pal!" Oh yes, he'd been paying attention alright, and at the tender age of three-and-a-half had already picked up my not altogether attractive habit of being an angry driver!)*

Far more recently, my grandson Elliot and my granddaughter Mya were at our house. Mya lives in a state of "Let's play and have fun!" She is constantly "suggesting" ideas of how other people might have the privilege of playing with *her*. Elliot, of course, usually is doing his best trying to ignore her. This time, finally she said to Elliot *(in a very controlling way)*, "Well then, let's play house. You can be the dad!" Elliot looked at her and conceded, "Okay." He promptly walked over to the table, pulled out a chair, sat in it, put up his feet, crossed his arms and as dad in their make-believe world declared, "I'm not doing anything because I've been working all day!" Hmmm… I wonder where he got that idea from?

CHILDREN ARE DESPERATE FOR ROLE MODELS

Treat Them Like an Audience

"The apple doesn't fall far from the tree," as they say, and boy are they right about that! Every once in a while—or maybe slightly more often than that, but I'm being generous here—I come across a kid so rude and so disrespectful, that it stuns me. Do you know what my very first thought is when this happens? *That kid's parents must be complete and total jerks.* I don't believe there are any truly bad children, but there are PLENTY of kids with bad parents doing all sorts of terrible things. It's not the kids who are failing and deserve the blame; it's the parents and the example they set. It reminds me of the little boy in country singer Rodney Atkins' song who uses a four-letter word after he spills his orange drink and fries. When Daddy asks him where he learned to talk like that, the proud tyke says, "I've been watching you." Don't kid yourself, those little eyes and ears are peeled to our every move.

Maybe in your own childhood your folks used the adage "do as I say, not as I do" *(think a slurred "Don't ever drink and drive - now top off my glass before we hit the road, and make it a stiff one.").*

> **DON'T KID YOURSELF, THOSE LITTLE EYES AND EARS ARE PEELED TO OUR EVERY MOVE.**

But we know better today. We are better. If we want our kids to grow into honest, respectful, grateful, *faithful* folk, we need to model those attributes as often and as completely as we humanly can. Skip the lectures and lead by example. That's the only part they're paying attention to anyway.

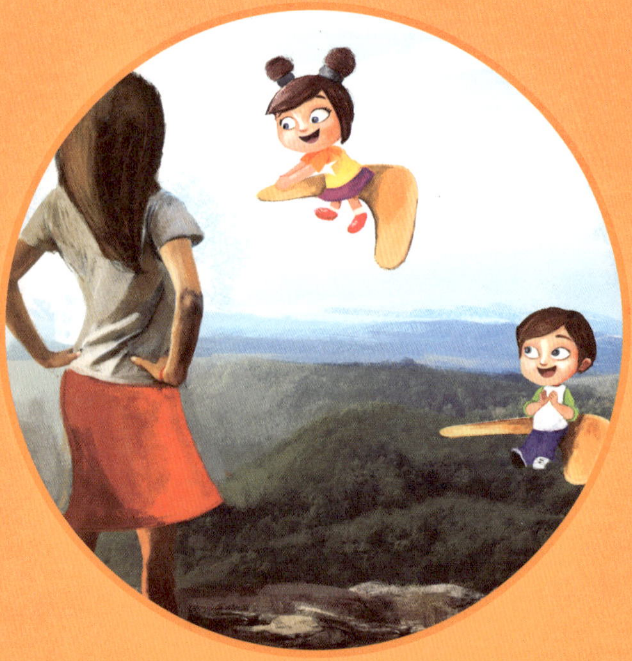

Treat Them Like Boomerangs

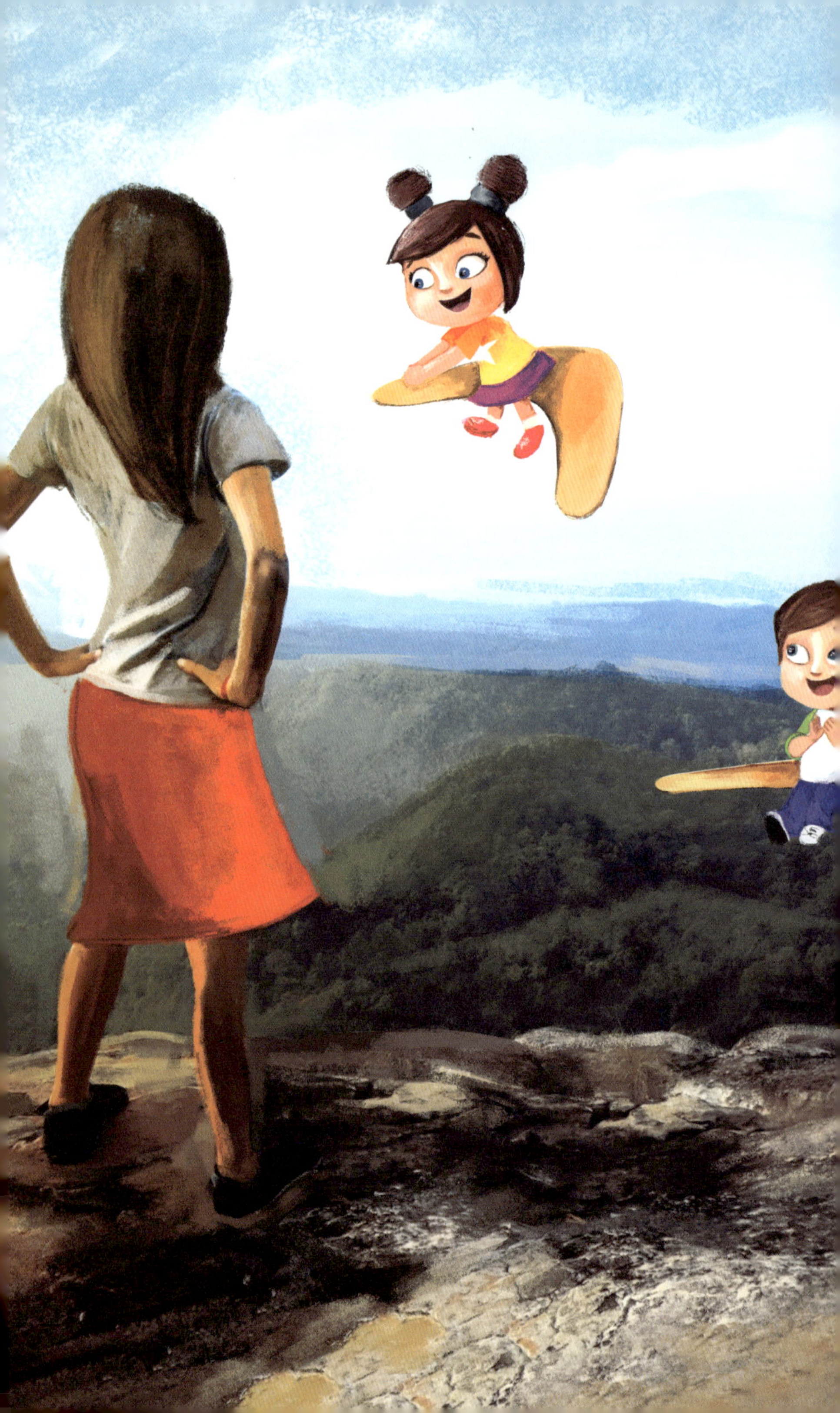

Treat Them Like Boomerangs

Imagine someone just gave you a boomerang for your birthday. And since odds are you aren't a boomerang expert and you probably aren't attached to this particular model seeing as it's brand new to you, let's imagine it's crafted of solid platinum and studded with giant diamonds and was signed by Elvis *and* Babe Ruth. Also, there's not another boomerang anything like it in the whole entire world.

This thing is worth a lot, is what I'm getting at here.

Now.

Would you in a million years dream of taking your brand new, absolutely priceless boomerang to the very top of the tallest mountain you could find and then chucking it off? If your answer to that question is "Why not? It's a boomerang! They always come back!" No offense, but you don't know squat about boomerangs.

Boomerangs were designed to come back *if the user knows what he's doing*. The path and the trajectory of that thing is entirely dependent on the skill of the thrower. If one were entrusted to the care of an extremely valuable boomerang, it would make sense then to work one's way gently into the sport; to practice relentlessly at getting better; to really put in the time before taking any great risks with it. Because if you let that thing sail without really knowing what you're doing, it's just not going to come back.

Kids are a lot like that. We get them when they're extremely small and their memories are lousy for a *reason*:

We don't know what the heck we're doing!

We get to make a million little mistakes without them being able to hold them all over our heads. We get to ever-so-slowly grant them greater freedoms, greater responsibilities, greater opportunities to screw up and learn from those lessons. The end goal, of course, is to let them fly... with the confident knowledge that they'll always come back.

Letting go isn't easy. It's not easy when they're thirteen months old and getting ready to take those first teetering steps, and it's not easy when they're eighteen years old and we're dropping them off at their college dorm. But I will tell you this: If you're still holding your eighteen-year-old's hand when he crosses the street, that college drop-off is going to be absolutely, unquestionably brutal. *(And by the way...you may have met one of those mothers who can't part from her brain-sucking toddler for even a well-deserved break. What's her deal? I mean, the woman is as stressed as she can be, she's overwhelmed by the constant neediness of this little organism she birthed, and she probably hasn't had a decent meal in months.*

But suggest, "Let's get a babysitter and go out on our own for a few hours..." and she freaks! "WHAT? Heavens no! I can't be away from my baby for a whole three hours!" Really? I'll bet both you and the kid would benefit greatly from a break. I know your husband certainly would! But again, I digress.)

> **THE END GOAL, OF COURSE, IS TO LET THEM FLY... WITH THE CONFIDENT KNOWLEDGE THAT THEY'LL ALWAYS COME BACK.**

Parenting really is such a delicate balance. We're built with this powerful urge to protect our children from harm, and yet we also know that experience is life's greatest teacher. The trick is finding that sweet spot where we can let our babies fall *(WITHOUT BREAKING ANYTHING*

OF COURSE) while we're still close enough to give them a hand getting back up.

A lot of parents have a hard time finding that sweet spot. *(These are often the ones you hear being called "helicopter parents.")* They pad corners when their kids are young and intervene in their every altercation when they're older. When little Jack is having a problem with little Joey in school, Helicopter Mom and Dad are on the phone to Joey's parents, the principal and anyone else who will listen before you can say *Dewy, Cheatem & Howe.* They bring ten-year-old Jack his lunch three times a week when he forgets it at home even though

TEN-YEAR-OLDS ARE FULLY CAPABLE OF REMEMBERING TO BRING THEIR LUNCHES

(but they never will if they don't have to).

Heli-Mom-and-Dad bail teenage Jack out of jail when he gets arrested for shoplifting, constantly badger his coach to play him more and are still fighting his every academic battle well into his college years.

> **WE'RE BUILT WITH THIS POWERFUL URGE TO PROTECT OUR CHILDREN FROM HARM, AND YET WE ALSO KNOW THAT EXPERIENCE IS LIFE'S GREATEST TEACHER.**

Truth be told, there's an exceptional chance thirty-three-year-old Jack will still be living with them or at least *off* of them, because he never managed to get himself an actual job. And then what do you suppose happens if Helicopter Mom and Dad choose THAT moment to say "We've had enough! It's time you grew up and learned to be independent. You're on your own!" Poor Jack doesn't have a prayer, does he? And it's not even his fault. He's like a boomerang that's been tossed off a cliff by an angry drunk... and I'm guessing he's about as likely to come back, too.

At our church in Green Bay, Wisconsin, we have a "gap year" program for graduating seniors. *[Visit TransitionOne.org]*

The idea is simple: Instead of graduating high school and dashing straight off to college, kids are encouraged to take a year off and put God first in their lives. They learn about faith, how to handle money, gain insights into choosing a spouse, learn how to become leaders, and experience serving and sacrifice. After six months of classroom study, they go overseas and serve for three months as temporary missionaries, feeding the hungry, helping the poor and having a positive influence on their host church or organization. What always shocks me is how many moms want to go and visit their offspring thirty days into their service.

Keep in mind, these are 18 to 21-year-old young men and women, not junior high school kids. And their mothers can't bear being away from them for more than thirty days?! *(The kids are usually fine with the separation, you won't be surprised to hear!)*

Children can't learn without making mistakes. And they can't make mistakes without being given some freedom to fail. They can't soar if we don't let them spread their wings. When we let our offspring deal with their own challenges, do you know what happens? *They learn to deal with their challenges!*

Proverbs 22:6 says,
"Teach your children to choose the right path, and when they are older, they will remain upon it."

And when you build your relationship with them on a solid foundation of guidance, respect and trust, they will always come back to you.

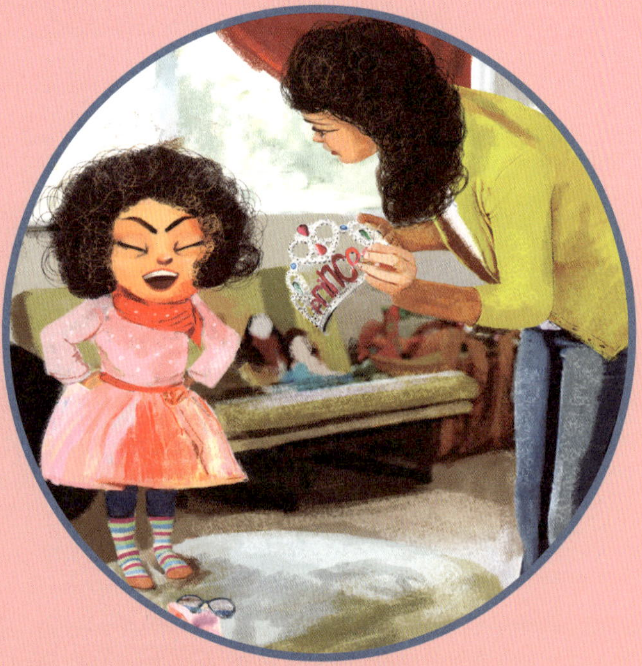

BONUS! Do NOT Treat Them Like Royalty

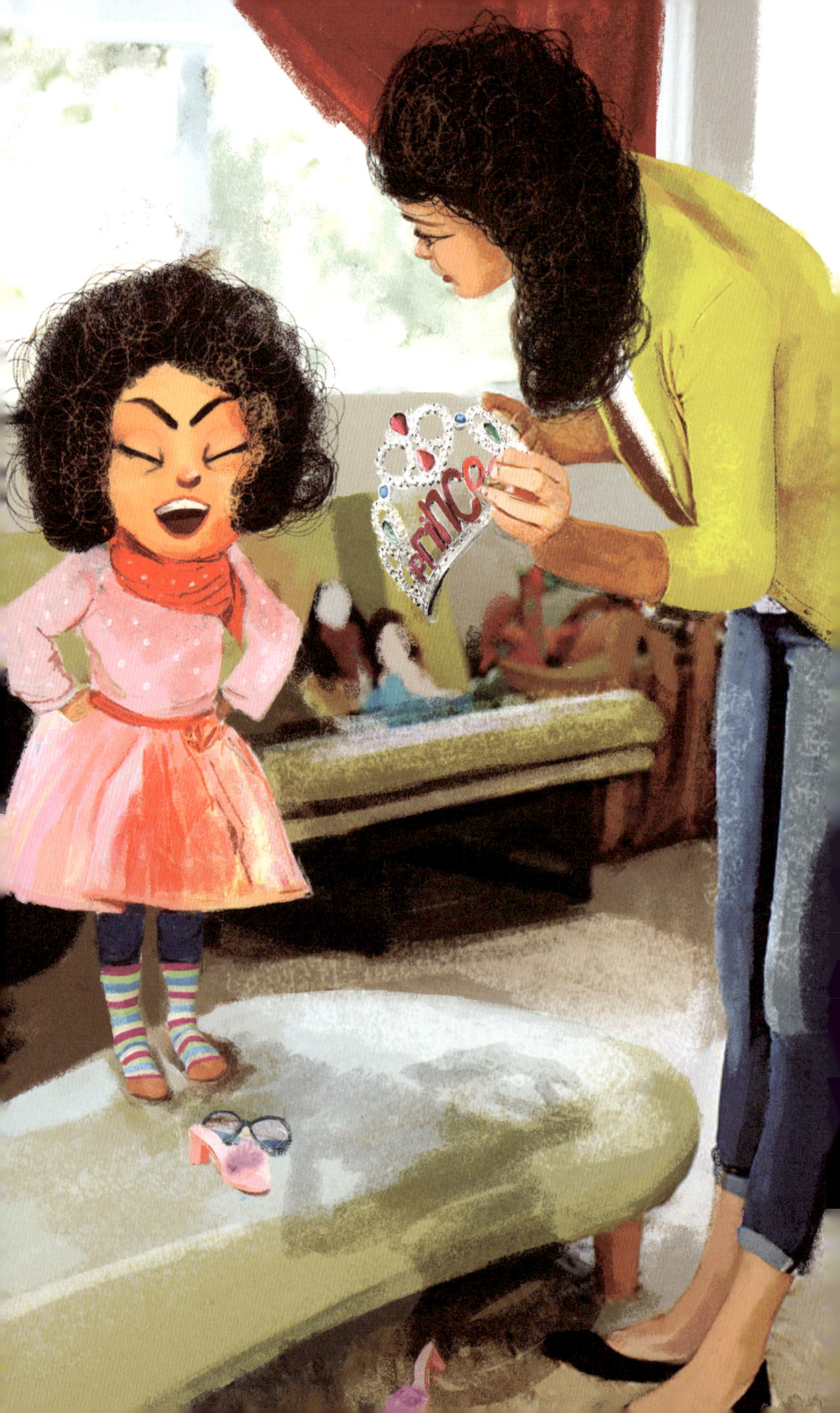

BONUS: Do NOT Treat Them Like Royalty

Once upon a time, in a galaxy far, far away, parents ruled their little kingdoms and kids did as they were told, without even questioning this (out loud at least). Parents made the rules, they *enforced* the rules, and I'd bet my last nickel not a single one of them ever smiled sweetly at their spawn before asking, "When you're finished what you are doing, would you like to come help me set the table?" Oh no. It was "Get your *[bleep]*

in here and set this table right this minute," and you were a lucky kid if there was a *please* on either end of that command.

We've come a long way, baby. Unfortunately, we've come a long way in the dangerously wrong direction in my *(rarely)* humble opinion.

I'm not saying we should go back to demanding swift and immediate compliance from our kids all day every day...Wait a minute: That's *exactly* what I'm saying! What was so bad about that? You wanted something done and it *got done!* You didn't want to hear any whining, and *you didn't hear any whining!* It was a fairly brilliant setup, if you ask me. So what happened?

Somewhere along the line, some lily-livered parents decided that we were crushing our children's little spirits every time we scolded them. We were limiting their potential with all our sweeping structure and niggling little rules. And frankly, the thinking went, *parenting would be a lot less stressful if we just gave our kids whatever the heck they wanted whenever the heck they wanted it.* Talk about conflict-free! **Yippy!**

Except.

As a parent, it's *your job* to set rules for your child—and then enforce those rules. Should you do this with love and compassion and respect? Absolutely! *But you need to do it.* If your little peanut doesn't learn to follow rules from you, what on earth will happen to her when she gets to school?

> **First grade teacher:** "Peanut, please sit on the rainbow carpet now for story time."
> **Peanut:** "I DON'T WANT TO AND YOU CAN'T MAKE ME!"
> **First grade teacher:** "Let's go ask Principal Pickapepper about that."
> *(Spoiler: Peanut gets detention.)*

What will happen when Peanut lands her first job?
> **Boss:** "File this stack of papers and return this list of phone calls."
> **Peanut:** "Oh, I don't like filing or making phone calls."

Boss: "I hope you like collecting unemployment then!"

Overly permissive parents usually defend themselves with the weakest argument on the planet: "My child *loves* my parenting style." Oh, I bet he does! Because you never say no to him! He gets to call all the shots—and what kid *(or adult for that matter)* wouldn't love that? What kid wouldn't want to be the king of his castle? But as Buddy the Elf said to the stand-in Santa, *he's sitting on a throne of lies.*

> **AS A PARENT, IT'S YOUR JOB TO SET RULES FOR YOUR CHILD—AND THEN ENFORCE THOSE RULES.**

In the 1960s and 1970s, a psychologist and professor by the name of Walter Mischel at Stanford University conducted a series of experiments on the delay of gratification in preschool children. His test basically went like this: "I'll give you a marshmallow and you can eat it right now. Or if you can wait fifteen minutes to eat it, I'll give you two marshmallows!" Predictably, seventy percent of the children ate the first marshmallow in advance of the fifteen-minute waiting period. *(A marshmallow in the hand and all...)*

A decade later, Mischel did a follow-up study using the same students he had tested originally. He discovered that the subjects' performance as four-year-olds had powerful implications ten years later. The four-year-olds who could delay gratification longer went on to achieve significantly higher SAT scores than the study participants who hadn't been able to delay their gratification. The disciplined group had also developed better social, cognitive and emotional coping skills.

Confident that the impacts of early self-restraint didn't stop there, Mischel revisited the same group again after they reached their 40s and 50s. As it turned out, the kids who had waited for two marshmallows those many years ago continued to excel in education, had a greater sense of self-worth, managed their stress better, and were less prone to abuse drugs and alcohol.

CONCLUSION OF THE STUDY: TEACH YOUR CHILDREN SELF-CONTROL.

Children of permissive parents who experience no consequences for their behavior are being set up for a host of problems as they get older. They tend to have poor social skills, lower academic achievement, and a difficult time dealing with authority. They're more likely to be overweight or obese and to experiment with drugs and alcohol at far earlier ages. Lack of structure leads to a lack of self-discipline and self-control, which are crucial skills for navigating adolescence and early adulthood.

The simple antidote? Do your job! You're not here to be your child's friend; he can and likely does have dozens of those! But he's only got two parents *(if he's lucky)*. As much as he might bristle when you lay down the law, the truth is children crave order; they thrive under firm, clear expectations.

> **YOU'RE NOT HERE TO BE YOUR CHILD'S FRIEND.**

Raising amazing kids is as much about what you ***don't do*** as what you ***do***:

Don't beg and plead with him to do the things you expect; your expectation should be enough.

Don't avoid conflict to preserve his mood; it's ***okay*** for kids to be upset every once in a while. These are some of the greatest teachable moments you will ever encounter.

Don't ask him if he'd like to leave the party or help you in the garden or take a nap if these are things you want him to do.

> **CHILDREN CRAVE ORDER; THEY THRIVE UNDER FIRM, CLEAR EXPECTATIONS.**

Remember, in this kingdom, you're the king, not him. The sooner you establish this as fact, the happier everyone in the kingdom will be.

More Treats

We hope you enjoyed TREAT THEM LIKE MONKEYS and that you feel like it's given you a fun new way to approach parenting.

If you'd like to employ some of the same simple, enjoyable strategies with your spouse, we've got you covered:

For *her*, there's TREAT HIM LIKE A DOG (don't worry, there are no leashes or poop bags involved!), and for *him*, we've got TREAT HER LIKE A TRUCK.

We're including the introductions to each on the following pages, so you'll have an idea of what's in store. Why not TREAT yourself? Here's to happily ever after!

markgungor.com

More from Gungor Publishing

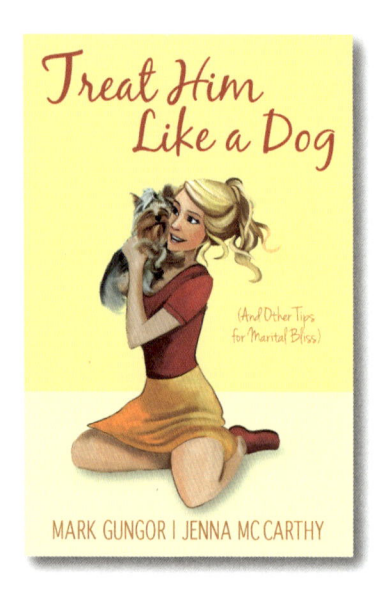

Introduction

Congratulations! You're now the proud owner of another book on relationships. We keep buying them because we want to succeed with the people closest to us. I should say, "Women keep buying them..." The truth is, most men would rather have root canal surgery or a rectal exam than read a book on relationships. Not that they don't need the help, and not that they wouldn't benefit from the wisdom and insight this book is teeming with. Oh, they neeeeeeed the help all right. But since it's the women

markgungor.com

Treat Him Like a Dog

who typically purchase and read relationship books, this work will be addressed to the fairer sex.

When you stood before that altar (the first draft of this work had a typo and the word was spelled 'alter'. I laughed and thought, "Oh, they're about to be altered alright...") or beside those gently lapping waves on that blinding white beach of your wedding-destination dreams, you said some version of the following:

> "I promise to love,
> honor and cherish
> you in sickness
> and in health,
> for richer or for poorer,
> for better or for worse,
> till death do us part."

You did! You said that!

As it turns out, till death do us part is a really looooong time—and being a loving, honoring, cherishing spouse all day every day is no easy feat. In

markgungor.com

fact, by most accounts it borders on the impossible. Not to mention that living with another person (which typically means sharing the same bed, the same bathroom and the same thermostat) has been known to try even the most temperate of tempers.

If you're among the very blessed, you're not bickering about the Big Things (namely money, sex and kids) on a daily basis. Most married couples admit that more often than not they find themselves arguing about tiny, trivial matters. Solomon once wrote:

> *A quarrelsome wife is like the dripping of a leaky roof in a rainstorm.*
> Proverbs 27:15 NIV

Granted, that was written from a man's perspective and there is conveniently no mention of the major pain in the rear that a husband can be, but the image of a dripping, leaky roof pretty much summarizes what life can be like after the "I Dos" have echoed off into the distant horizon.

He left crumbs in the sink again! He forgot

markgungor.com

Treat Him Like a Dog

to pick up the dry cleaning like you asked him to! And who puts the empty milk carton back in the refrigerator, anyway? These are just a few from the long list of transgressions he commits on a continual basis as he demonstrates his skillful ability to descend into pig-like behavior. Drip, drip, drip.

The truth is, many of us –men included— willingly (sometimes even eagerly) pick a fight with our spouses over some petty thing that if it were committed by almost anyone else in the world, we'd graciously let it slide. That's what dripping will do to you.

Part of the problem is that pesky living-together-business. When you're confined to a small space (relative to the rest of the planet, let's say), the people who share that space with you get front row seats to your every emotional extreme: They are there to witness your rapturous highs (You got the promotion! Your hair looks amazing today!) and your heartbreaking lows (Your beloved dog has to be put down! You gained four pounds on your diet!). The highs often go by without a lot of fanfare, but those lows? They kick you in the butt every time.

markgungor.com

Treat Him Like a Dog

Here's why: Just for fun, let's look at the dying-dog scenario. (After all, nothing lifts the spirits like a lively discussion about the death of the family pet.)

Seriously, tragic things happen in our lives on a discouragingly regular basis. But you still have to show up at work, and maybe attend a PTA meeting, and possibly meet with the accountant or play another rousing game of Candy Land, and essentially do all manner of challenging, grown-up things that require you to keep it together when inside you're a miserable mess.

So you do—you keep it together brilliantly, in fact. At least until you get home. And then you fall apart, because you're not a machine and sometimes you have to let it out. (After all, you miss that stupid dog - that dog that regularly added to your already heavy work load each and every day.) And who's left staring at the broken pieces of you and scratching his head as to how to begin to put you back together again? No, it's not all the king's horses and all the king's men; it's that person you promised to love, honor and cherish every single day for the rest of ever. (Honestly! What were you thinking?)

markgungor.com

Treat Him Like a Dog

Here's the thing: We're not bad people; far from it. We're human. We have value. God loves us all. (How and why, I'll never understand. I mean, let's face it, this would be a great planet if it weren't for people.) And it's human nature to take things for granted. There's actually a scientific name for it—hedonic adaptation—but I'll spare you the psychology lecture. The bottom line is that we don't appreciate the things that become commonplace in our lives.

For instance, being able to sit painlessly at a desk until you throw out your back and get laid up for a week. Or when was the last time you gave your thumb a second thought? Slice that thing open with your sharpest butcher knife and have it bandaged up for a month and I guarantee, you'll be grateful to have it back. How about breathing? Inhale, exhale, inhale, exhale; you do it all day long, never considering the fact that your hardworking respiratory system is very busy keeping you alive while you're off playing tennis and surfing the Internet or steaming broccoli.

So it goes with your husband. Sure you love him, in the vague and all-encompassing sense of the word. You honor him, especially when he takes out the trash without being asked. You try your best to cherish him, even when his snoring wakes you up for the third time in a single night. But you don't always appreciate him—and he certainly doesn't always get the best version of you.

    How can he, when there's a big, demanding world out there that wants—often needs—more than you've got to give in the first place? Think of your time, attention and affection as a glorious holiday meal to which you've invited pretty much everyone in your entire contact list. You get dressed to the nines, polish a truckload of silver and then heap their plates high, because you're a gracious hostess and it's what you've been taught to do. You smile and you make polite chitchat as you serve your parade of hungry guests. Hours pass. Your lipstick is long gone and your feet are beginning to throb and all you want is for this party to end and these people to go home. At the very end of the line is your husband. He's starving; he's lonely; he's missed you all day. But you're exhausted, out of food, and your face hurts from smiling. If he's lucky, you might toss

markgungor.com

him the nearly naked turkey carcass to pick over before you hobble into bed.

If it were but one giant holiday meal a year where your husband got the sad leftovers, it would be one thing. But many wives are living that scenario day in and day out. If you are like most women, you smile at strangers on the street all day long, praise your kids for every scribbled stick person they draw and fawn over your dog for lifting a lousy paw. (Of course I just had to remind you of the stupid dead dog.) Think your husband wouldn't like a piece of that action? Think again. I know, you're already giving till it hurts. But sometimes it's good to step back and take a look at some of the people and things in your life that get the sort of time and attention from you that your husband would give his eyeteeth to enjoy.

It's also crucial to understand that what is the most important doesn't always get the most time. For example, we've all heard the standard priority list: God first, then spouse, children and work. Sounds about right. But think about it – you actually spend the most time working, family gets your next biggest allotment, your spouse gets crumbs (until the kids grow up and finally leave) and God? Well, who prays eight hours a day? Still, the priority list is right. But you see, it's not about the amount of time – it's about quality and devotion. Since what is most important actually ends up with the least amount of our time, it is up to us to make sure that time matters.

So, since this book is dedicated to sharing simple bits of advice about how you can continue to care for and cherish that man you pledged your heart to and because I don't want you to be traumatized for life, I'll start with your healthy, happy dog. (The dead dog analogy was getting old anyway...)

More from Gungor Publishing

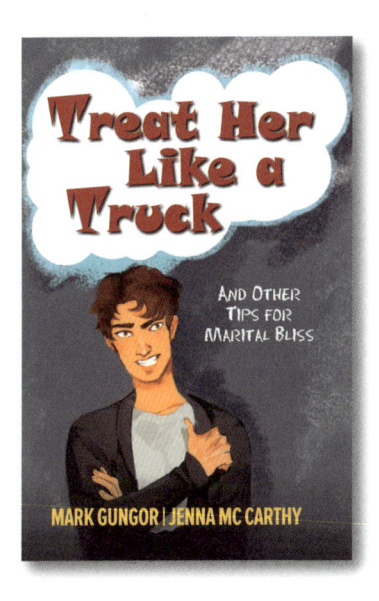

Treat Her Like a Truck
And Other Tips for Marital Bliss
MARK GUNGOR | JENNA MC CARTHY

Introduction

Congratulations! You're now the proud owner of a book on relationships. I'll bet this has been on your wish list for years, possibly decades. Is that the sound of you tap-dancing I hear? Or was that a champagne cork popping? After all, the only thing men love even more than talking about their feelings is reading about them, am I right?

I'll be here all week!

Obviously, I jest. The fact that you've gotten to this third paragraph, frankly, could be considered one of those "everyday miracles" some

markgungor.com

folks use to prove God exists. So, let me tell you right up front that even though this technically is a relationship book, I promise you it's unlike any other you've ever encountered—or more likely, any you've dreaded encountering. For one thing, I'm not going to give you painful exercises to perform or ask you to delve deep into your psyche/past/wallet to figure out why you're so emotionally constipated. Besides, explaining why a man is emotionally constipated is pretty easy: It's because you're a man! It's how God designed you, and I'm pretty sure he had a darned good reason for doing it that way. Likewise, he designed your wife the way she is for a reason, too, which may or may not be slightly neater, fresher-smelling and needier than you are, emotionally and conversationally.

    Did God construct men craving high speeds in a car with rolled-down windows and give women blinding white knuckles and the skills to create complicated hairstyles that immediately fall apart when said window is rolled down just so we could drive each other insane until death finally separates us? No, these differences were never designed to drive us crazy. He designed us differently so we could complement one another; learn from and grow with; someone who makes us whole.

And then drives us nuts.

Why do we do this thing called marriage? Why are we so powerfully drawn to someone so different from ourselves, even though at times it can be so completely frustrating?

Well, beyond the obvious reason of sexual attraction, the truth is, we are better with that woman than we are without her.

The wise King Solomon once wrote:
Two are better than one, because they have
a good return for their labor:
If either of them falls down,
one can help the other up.
But pity anyone who falls
and has no one to help them up.
Also, if two lie down together, they will
keep warm.
But how can one keep warm alone?
Though one may be overpowered,
two can defend themselves.
Ecclesiastes 4:9-12 (NIV)

markgungor.com

Treat Her Like a Truck

If you're like most men, you probably feel like you're a pretty good husband, all things considered. You're not perfect, but you definitely love your wife, and you're certainly committed to her. So why does it sometimes feel like you can't make her happy?

The ironic answer is, because you're married to her!

See, if you'd intended to remain a bachelor for the rest of ever, my "how to be happy" advice would be completely different. I'd tell you to go ahead and fart in the car with the windows up, drink properly chilled bottles of beer while you watch ESPN around the clock, and let your nose hairs grow down to your chin if you happen to like that look. I would give you permission to never, ever watch another chick flick as long as you live, and encourage you to drag your hamper to the curb and start leaving your dirty boxers and socks scattered about your home like confetti. But if you're reading this book (and by that, I probably mean if your wife is making you read this book), I'd bet my last nickel you're no bachelor—or if you are, you won't be one for long. No, you are half of a whole, and you've got someone else to think about now. Someone else with ideas, wants, needs, and movie preferences vastly different from your own. And it may be a fuzzy memory today, but when you stood before that altar or beside those gently lapping waves on that blinding white beach of your bride's wedding-destination dreams, you said some version of the following:

"I promise to love, honor and cherish you in sickness and in health, for richer or for poorer, for better or for worse, till death do us part."

(You did! You said that!)

As it turns out, till death do us part is a really looooong time—and being a loving, honoring, cherishing partner all day every day is no easy feat. In fact, by most accounts it borders on the impossible. Not to mention that living with another person (which typically means sharing the same bed, the same bathroom and the same thermostat) has been known to try even the most temperate of tempers.

If you're among the very blessed, you're not bickering about the Big Things (namely money, sex and kids) on a daily basis. Most married couples admit that more often than not they find themselves arguing about tiny, trivial matters.

Solomon also once wrote:

A quarrelsome wife is like the dripping of a leaky roof in a rainstorm.

- Proverbs 27:15 (NIV)

Granted, that was written from a man's perspective and there is conveniently no mention of the major pain in the rear that a husband can be, but the image of a dripping, leaky roof pretty much summarizes what life can be like after the "I Dos" have echoed off into the distant horizon.

I bet you'd like to plug that leak, wouldn't you? I bet you'd give up your favorite hobby for, like six months, maybe even a year, to have an airtight wife.

Here's the thing: You can! And it's not even that hard!

You: Oh, here you go. You're going to tell me I have to change.

Me: No I'm not. I'm really, truly not.

You: Mark, I don't believe you! How can I make my wife happy without changing? She doesn't even like me!

Treat Her Like a Truck

Of course, you're skeptical. I don't blame you, especially if you're married to a woman who occasionally or even frequently points out how miserable you make her. (All women do this, incidentally. Oh, they don't do it to be mean; they do it because they like to communicate. And they actually believe that if they tell us something they don't like about our personalities or behavior, that we'll actually change it! Bless their innocent, hopeful little hearts…) But you really can make her happy, and you can do it simply by continuing to do what you've done all along…with every other person and thing in your life.

Think about that lovely little lady you married for a minute. Sure, you love her, in the vague and all-encompassing sense of the word. You honor her (especially when she makes flank steak or doesn't turn down your request for a little morning action.) You try your best to cherish her, even when she insists on giving you a real-time play by play of her day when all you asked was how it was, and all you wanted to hear was "great." But you know it and I know it: You don't always

markgungor.com

appreciate her—and she certainly doesn't always get the best version of you.

Don't tell her I said this, but sometimes she's sort of like that hideous recliner chair you love so much. She's comfortable, she's dependable, and you probably wouldn't even notice if somebody spilled a bowl of chili on her. (Okay, you probably would notice that...and post a picture of it on Facebook.) But in a nutshell, you mostly take her for granted.

You: You lied! You said I didn't have to change!

Me: Relax. I didn't lie. You really don't have to change.

The super-easy-secret-trick to making your wedded wife happy is to behave the way you've always behaved—around your car, your television, your tool box, even your old baseball glove. I know, you think I sound crazy right now, but that's not important. What's important is that you're reading a relationship book, and you're enjoying it, and you're going to keep reading it because you have my word that you do not have to change.

Treat Her Like a Truck

All you have to do is start treating her less like your old recliner and more like some of the other things in life that you love. It really is that easy.

Let's do this.

More from Mark

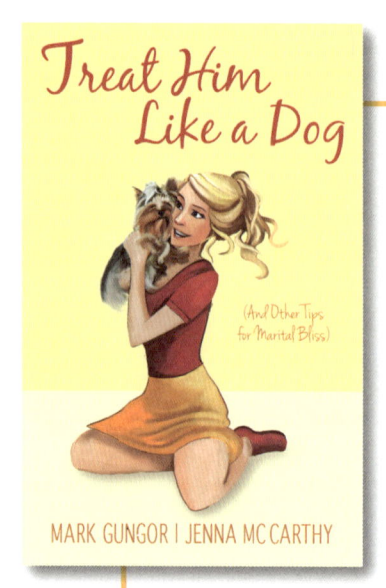

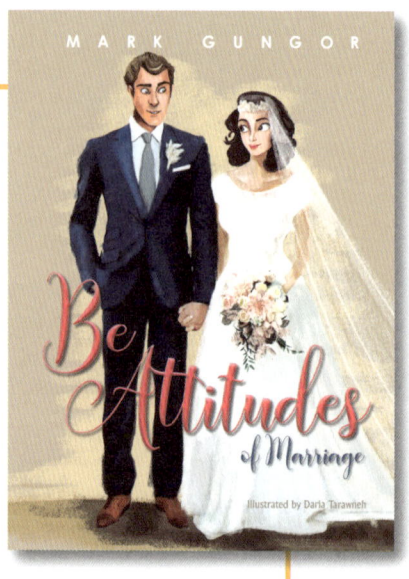

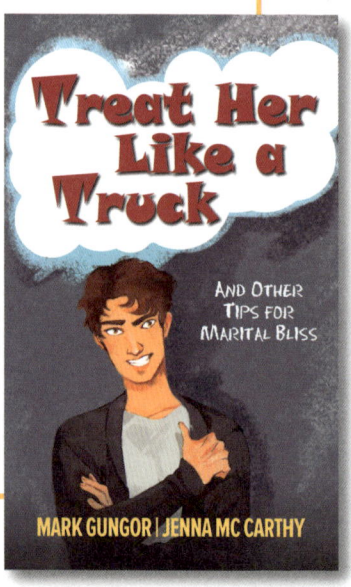

Treat Him Like a Dog (And Other Tips for Marital Bliss)
MARK GUNGOR | JENNA MC CARTHY

MARK GUNGOR — Be Attitudes of Marriage
Illustrated by Darla Tarawneh

Treat Them Like Monkeys
MARK GUNGOR • JENNA MCCARTHY

Treat Her Like a Truck And Other Tips for Marital Bliss
MARK GUNGOR | JENNA MC CARTHY

markgungor.com

More from Mark

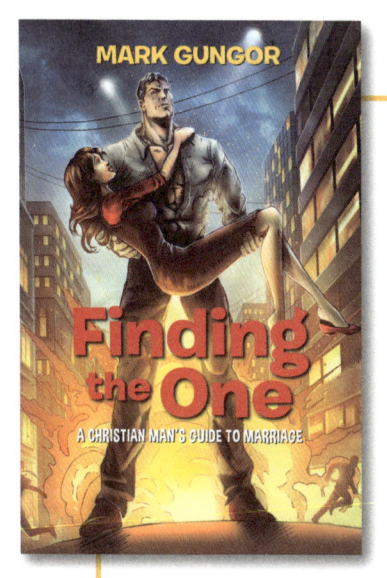

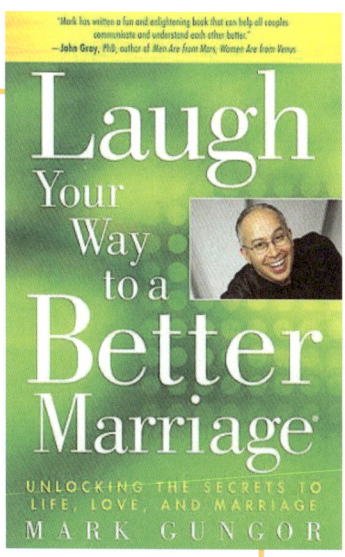

Finding the One
A Christian Man's Guide to Marriage
Mark Gungor

Laugh Your Way to a Better Marriage
Unlocking the Secrets to Life, Love, and Marriage
Mark Gungor

The Battle Over the Rules
Mark Gungor
Illustrations by Alfredo Montané Vargas

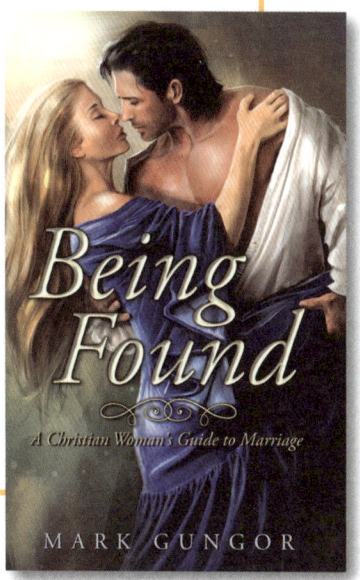

Being Found
A Christian Woman's Guide to Marriage
Mark Gungor

markgungor.com

More from Mark

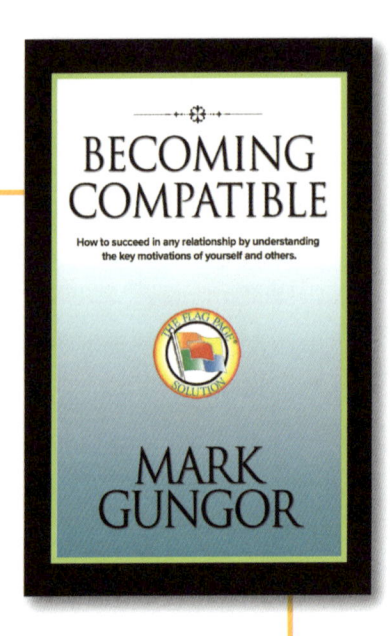

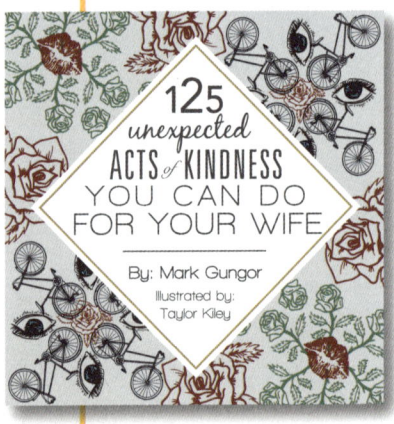

markgungor.com

About the Author

MARK GUNGOR is one of the most sought-after international speakers on marriage and family and is author of the best-selling book Laugh Your Way to a Better Marriage. Mark and his wife De Anna make their home in Green Bay, Wisconsin. You can learn more about Mark at www.markgungor.com.

markgungor.com